Many Blessings Will Come

"Through case stories, Kemila Zsange, RCCH takes the reader on an intimate journey into healing through hypnotherapy, past life regressions, and in-between life memories. With clear explanations and deep empathy, the author captures our hearts and attention with engaging accounts. Highly recommend for those curious about spiritual regressions and the healings that can occur."

— Heather S. Friedman Rivera, R.N., J.D, Ph.D.,
author of *Healing the Present from the Past:*
The Personal Journey of a Past Life Researcher

"Kemila Zsange's book, *MANY BLESSINGS WILL COME*, contains numerous case summaries of clients whose current lives improved as a result of a past life regression (PLR). Although some people are skeptical of past life regressions and hypnotic techniques to induce them, sometimes we need to consider new paradigms. Even skeptical therapists may facilitate past life regressions when requested because they find that even if the PLR was a fantasy or a memory channeled from the 'other side', it usually benefited the client. You will find some of the case summaries in Kemila's book are truly amazing."

— Roy Hunter, DAPHP, DIMDHA,
Published Author, Hypnosis Instructor

"The blessings and answers are already here, waiting to be discovered. Kemila Zsange's third book Many Blessings Will Come is a testament to her inspired approach to hypnotherapy, her brilliant talent as a storyteller, and her unending willingness to dive deep into the abyss of the subconscious mind. The stories in this beautifully written compilation are the real-life accounts of her clients' very personal, experiential journeys into healing, recovery of self, and the gifts and wisdom brought into their lives by them bravely exploring their past, future, and in-between lives. This book, written with compassion, grace, sensitivity and eloquence, is sure to move the soul of anyone who has a desire to open their minds and explore possibilities of their consciousness in this wild ride we call life."

– Korë Jackson, RCCH,
Aquarian Deva Universal & Kore Intuitive

"With a treasure trove of fascinating past life stories, Kemila paints a lucid map of soul journeys, each shining with wonder and intrigue and merging into a river of light and wholeness. This unique perspective of lived experiences provides the clarity and wisdom necessary for healing and enlightenment."

– Bei Linda Tang,
author of *Navigate Life with Dreams*
and founder of Dream Heals *dreamheals.org*

"Kemila's soothing and reassuring guidance takes us on a spiritual journey through other planes of existence to unveil the complex nature of the Soul experience. This remarkable collection of magical stories makes a compelling case that many of our current conflicts and reservations are rooted in past lives while resoundingly proving that our salvation is possible through strengthening connections with our soulmates and re-claiming our unique talents. Each story is a profound journey of personal transformation, yet relatable to anyone, regardless of spiritual beliefs, demonstrating possible paths to higher healing and closure. A humble yet eloquent portrayal of painful human quests makes an easy and enjoyable read for everyone who strives to grasp the complexity of their Soul's journey."

– Alexander Formos,
poet, author of *The World of Holly*

"Many Blessings Will Come is a blessing in itself. Each client's journey into, between and through lifetimes is captured in colourful detail and curated by Kemila's discerning and signature 'curious eye'. While mining the wisdom residing in the lifetimes of each of her clients, although it was primarily for them, I found that it has simultaneously provided insight for me, the reader, as I make sense of and learn about my own experience. It will be of interest to professionals in this field and laypeople alike."

– Lucca Hallex,
Power Sourcerer, Psychic & Medium
www.powersourcerer.com

Kemila Zsange

MANY BLESSINGS WILL COME

OTHER JOURNEY BEYOND BOOKS BY KEMILA ZSANGE

Carol's Lives ~
Two Soul's Journey in Two Cities and Beyond

Past Life Regression ~
A Manual for Hypnotherapists to Conduct Effective Past
Life Regression Sessions

Available at www.kemilahypnosis.com/online-store
on www.amazon.com or *anywhere books are*

Kemilahypnosis   @kemilahypnosis

@kemilahypnosis   Kemila Zsange

www.kemilahypnosis.com

MANY BLESSINGS WILL COME

Tales of Recovering Inner Commitments,
Gifts, and Wisdom Through
Hypnotherapy

KEMILA ZSANGE

JOURNEY BEYOND PRODUCTIONS

A Journey Beyond Book
Published by Journey Beyond Productions
A division of Kemila Zsange Hypnotherapy & Counselling
Vancouver, Canada

This work is a true account of actual events. Some dialogue and characteristics have been altered or supplemented for dramatic purposes. All persons within are actual individuals; there are no composite characters. All individuals' names and identifying features have been changed to respect their privacy.

Paperback, First Edition 2022, Journey Beyond Production
Cover design by Linda Stelluti
Edited by Melanie Christian
Printed and bound in Canada

ISBN: 978-1-7775089-4-4

To my mother, Luo Hui Wen
I have never made it into a mission for you to be proud of me, but it has
been incredibly gratifying knowing that you are. I know you will read
this book in Heaven.

Contents

Forward

Since the very beginning of our existence, humans have struggled with the meaning of life.

Age-old questions of "Who am I?", "Where do I come from?" and "What is my soul's purpose?" rummage through our mind like a child looking for their favorite toy.

As a clinical hypnotherapist, I connected deeply with Kemila Zsange's book, *Many Blessings Will Come*, and the emotional impact it has for those seeking answers to these timeless questions.

Based on fascinating past, future, and inter- life stories from actual clients, each chapter takes the reader on an amazing journey through time and space demonstrating the intriguing possibility of reincarnation–a belief that there is life after death.

With profound insights into the spiritual realm, Kemila shares some of her most captivating hypnotherapy sessions with respect, kindness, and a gentle approach for inner healing.

In order to understand the concept of past lives and source energy, she beautifully states:

"Every life and personality are akin to a single drop of water in a vast ocean; it is truest to itself and flows best when still connected to the greater whole. Unlike drops of water, humans when separated from their whole self, develop fears, self-doubt, and can become stuck or stagnant. The water droplet never stops being the ocean, we only perceive it as something separate when it is physically not

in the ocean. Coming home to the ocean, the drop of water
loses form, once again flowing in constant harmony with
the whole."

In our profession, we are often asked about the
relevancy of our work and how do we know, for a fact,
that information revealed in spiritual regression is real.

The truth is… we don't.

We don't know whether the subconscious mind is
making up stories while under a hypnotic state or if we
are truly tapping into a deeper part of memories in our
psyche. The real question that should be pondered is
this…

Does it really matter?

If the door to the greater unknown opens and a
catharsis occurs, traumatic pain is released or an
epiphany is revealed, shouldn't that be the triumph?

The famous psychologist Carl Jung embraced the
theory of reincarnation, but could not state it openly or
be subject to ridicule by the psychoanalytical
community.

He developed the concept of the "collective
unconscious", that which is made up of a collection of
knowledge and imagery that every person is born with
and is shared by all human beings due to ancestral
experience.

Like Jung, Kemila Zsange stretches the outskirts of
conventional philosophy to help one attain their own
wisdom.

I believe we are all here on this planet to
"experience" life itself – in all of its pain, glory, love,

heartbreak, and death. To have it any other way would be boring.

As a kindred soul, I give thanks to Kemila for her dedication to the field of hypnotherapy and wholeheartedly recommend *Many Blessings Will Come* to anyone who loves to go beyond the norm and delve into the mystery of the unknown.

Who knows… maybe we were Egyptian sisters in a past life!

Michele Guzy, C.Ht.
"The Mind Coach"
Hypnotherapist / Past Life Regression Specialist / Media Host

Introduction

Over the years in my hypnotherapy practice, I have met with people from many cultures, age groups, and all walks of life. It continues to be a profound and sacred journey working with them all. I feel indescribably lucky and incredibly honoured to have walked this healing path with so many, many souls.

I have always been fond of writing—from my younger days writing travel stories for magazines to writing a manual, a memoir, and now documenting case stories from my hypnotherapy practice in this book.

In a traditional sense, my work is "trance work." I create a state we call hypnotic trance during hypnotherapy, where people may access their innermost subconscious memories. These memories can extend beyond this lifetime, holding wisdom from beyond time itself.

Listening to all the stories, insights, and intuition my clients have shared and the knowledge they receive while in a trance state, I am glimpsing a kind of universal truth and wisdom, something that can awaken us all to our true nature of existence. I wonder, then, why would we call that hypnotic trance state an "altered" state of consciousness? It feels more faithful to our true nature than our "normal" waking state.

From the beginning of my studies, where my instructors' sole focus was on behavioural modification and emotional stability benefits and practices, I possessed a keen interest in using hypnosis to support people in waking from the trance of their everyday lives. I know this sounds like a paradox, using one trance to wake from another, but as many of the stories in this book will show, paradoxes can support us in waking up from the trance of suffering.

Traditional methods of studying behaviour and the mind are limited to singular experiences. They assume all action and reaction within your environment is limited to the current linear life on which we are focused. Past Life Regression, or PLR, as demonstrated in many of the stories in this book, offers access to answers to seemingly unanswerable questions in our current life. The results bring forth greater clarity to individuals who might otherwise be unable to access these more profound and practical truths beyond their singular life experiences.

With traditional psychology, parents can easily be blamed as the root cause of an issue. In past life regression therapy, so may past lives be similarly blamed. Both can serve to justify things going wrong in one's present lifetime. Blaming a past life can be comforting to a person: I did wrong three lifetimes ago, and now I am paying the price and atoning for those sins. Countless times, I have heard, "I must have hurt others in a past life, so now I am being hurt in this lifetime." Or "I took financial advantage of others before in past lifetimes, so now my lot in life is to suffer financially." People call it karma.

As both a therapist and a facilitator of past life regression experiences, it is vitally important to help people find empowerment through their past, present, future, and life between lives experiences. Blaming anyone or anything, be it parents or past lives, can never serve to heal and empower. Who we are right now is who we ARE. We are not a progression but a composition of our past lives. We need not find convenient excuses for not being who we want to be. The information we receive through spiritual regression experiences is to gain better insight, empowerment, and awareness into our life choices. Even though we use regressions as a tool to do so, a key focus of the stories in this book is taking responsibility for oneself in the current moment.

Healing is always in the now. Despite that, in regression, we assume we are dealing with memories from a so-called past. The Future is imagination, but how do we know the Past is not also imagination? Now is all that matters.

Storytelling is by nature linear, but lives are not. Time as a universal truth does not exist. As you read the stories in this book, you will find yourself jumping backward and forward in time. From the first telling of these stories to the time when they occurred. From a present life to a parallel one or one that happened in a different place and time. I hope that as you become accustomed to the rhythm of these stories, the shifts in time-space perspective begin to feel more natural to you.

Due to time constraints, only a tiny fraction of my sessions get written. Yet, all these stories have taken place. All clients whose accounts are presented here have given me prior permission to publish them. Their names have been changed, as have identifying details.

I use the terms "subconscious mind" and "unconscious mind" interchangeably throughout this book. I mostly prefer using "unconscious mind," but in some cases, the term "subconscious mind" may better fit the flow of the story.

It is a widespread practice with members of my profession that as our work deepens, we desire to create more group work, seminars, courses, and workshops. I have not yet grown out of the joy of working with people one on one.

There is so much in it for me when I journey with a willing mind and a curious soul. Writing this book for the general public and hypnotherapy professionals may well be my way of "reaching more people." I do not know what the future holds for me, but at the time of writing and publishing this book, I remain joyously seeing clients on a one-on-one basis.

For more information on my private hypnotherapy practice, additional case stories, hypnosis manuals and audios, please visit my website: www.kemilahypnosis.com. For my other books, visit www.carolslives.com.

Kemila Zsange
August 2022

Part 1: Recovering Inner Commitments

Past Life Relationships and Friendships Brought Forth in This Life

RECOVER verb (used with object)
- to get back or regain something lost or taken away.
- to make up for or make good (e.g., oneself, loss, damage, etc.).
- to regain strength, composure, balance, or the like (e.g., oneself).
- to reclaim from a bad state, practice, etc.
- to regain (a substance) in usable form, as from refuse material or a waste product or by-product of manufacture; reclaim.

verb (used without object)
- to regain health after being sick, wounded, or the like (often followed by from):
- to regain a former and better state or condition:
- to regain one's strength, composure, balance, etc.

A Prior Engagement

Assumptions Create Misery

I had just asked Imogen if I could write about her story in my book. It had not taken her long to answer. Shrugging casually, she had replied, "Yes. You can even use my real name. I have nothing to hide."

I looked at her, "I'd say the same thing if I were asked."

But I did change her name and identifying details, as I have done with all my clients whose stories, I have received permission to share.

Imogen was a young woman about half my age, yet it felt effortless communicating with her from the very beginning. She told me that she was going to write a book about dating based on her own experiences.

When I asked Imogen what she wanted to work on, she answered that she felt lonely and spoke of her fear of being alone. Five years earlier, she had broken up with her boyfriend of the time. She had not had much luck finding romance since then. She had trust issues and did not feel safe with anyone.

At that time, I was going through significant emotional stress in my own life. Unexpectedly, it became essential for me to move, quite abruptly, to a new office. The move was very inconvenient for many of my clients, and the sudden transition took its toll on me. I shared with Imogen that although it was her first session with me, it was also my last session practicing from that location. I did not even know why I emphasized that, but it felt significant.

Imogen's ease helped me. She explained that the therapist she regularly saw was unable to help her identify anything that related to or could explain her fear. "In this life at least," she hinted.

My curiosity sufficiently piqued, I looked at her and asked, "You would like to have a past life regression? Is that right?"

"Yes," she replied eagerly, with her eyes shining bright. Imogen continued, describing a past life regression experience she had a year earlier to alleviate her fear of heights and water.

"Did it work?"

"Yes. It worked! And it was also incredibly intriguing to see what the connections with my family members were in those past lives."

Having a previous successful experience in therapeutic past life regression, I knew Imogen would make my work with her relatively easy. And once she had settled comfortably on the couch, I had her relax, reach out, and get in touch with her fear of being alone. Together, we invited that pervasive presence in Imogen's life, fear itself, to come and join us and tell us its tale.

Imogen found herself in a male's life, Karan. He was in his mid-twenties, the same as Imogen. The young man stood, well-dressed, in the middle of a large garden or forest.

"I'm not certain of the location. I see trees," Karan-Imogen explained as he was describing his surroundings.

A past life regression can often start rather vaguely. There may be indistinct impressions, but commonly there is no clear concept of who a person is or what is happening when it begins.

"You can become aware of the temperature of your emotions. How are you feeling standing there amongst the trees?" A key to someone moving forward in regression is not to assume and to use only the information that has been given.

"I feel curious. I am…" Karan hesitated, "…Looking for something." I asked Karan to move forward to the moment when he either found what he had been seeking or no longer believed he would find it.

"No. I haven't found…" again, Karan hesitated, "…It's a person I am looking for."

"Would that be a he or she?"

"She!"

"How do you feel when you don't find her?"

"I feel sad. We were supposed to meet here. But she hasn't shown up."

"Who is she?" I tapped on the back of Imogen's hand, both for emphasis and to distract her conscious mind. "You know this."

"She's a girl from the other village. And I *love* her."

Karan had met this "girl from the other village" at a market a year before. She was pretty with long dark hair, fair skin, and a radiant smile. And her eyes! She had the most unforgettable, beautiful eyes Karan had ever seen.

However, a dark shroud hung over the young lovers' romance. Much like Shakespeare's Montagues and Capulets, their villages were sworn enemies. In their yearlong, furtive courtship, the couple lived in constant fear of being discovered by their rival villages. I inwardly sighed, how many real-life Romeo-and-Juliet love stories had there been throughout human history, tragic tales of love strewn across different families, countries, cultures, and eras? I wondered why individual human relations needed to be of larger societal concern. And when would we truly learn to accept and honour the simple harmonies of love?

"So, she didn't show up," I continued, guiding the expansion of the story. "That means something. It might mean she didn't want to see you anymore. Or she couldn't. You don't know, do you?"

"No, I don't," Karan replied hopelessly. "But I'm crying nonetheless."

"When you have cried enough, what do you do next?"

"I just sit there. And wait. What if she comes? What if she is just late for some reason?"

"How long do you stay there and wait?"

"I sit there and wait the whole night, looking in the direction from which she was supposed to come. The direction of the river."

It was apparent this was a harrowing experience for Karan. Eventually, though, Karan had to leave. After waiting for his love all night, he was both tired and hungry, and his parents, sister, brother, and grandmother, with whom he lived, would be missing him. But surely, Karan thought bitterly, not as much as he was missing his "girl from the other village."

Two years after Karan's failed rendezvous, his parents arranged for him to marry a woman of their choosing and from their village. That marriage brought forth two children. Karan proved to be a dutiful husband, and his wife[1] a kind and caring mother and partner.

Yet, Karan could never forget the memory of the girl with the beautiful eyes.

---

[1] Much to Imogen's surprised delight, Karan's wife turned out to be Imogen's mother in her current life.

For many years following that heartbreaking day by the river, Karan held an inner dialogue with his past lover. Over and over and over again, he asked, pleading, "Why did you not show up?" Questions were all that Karan had, for he would never see that girl again for the remainder of his life.

Over time, Karan learned to bury his despair in a place deep inside himself. He lived an ordinary life working as a merchant, content with his wife and watching his children grow and start their own families.

I brought Karan forward again in that life: at 87 years of age, he lay on his deathbed surrounded by his children and grandchildren; his wife had passed away several years earlier. When asked what his last thought was, he replied it was still and always of the girl with the unforgettable eyes.

"Looking back and knowing what you know now, would you have done anything differently?"

"I would have spoken with someone from her village and found out why she never showed up."

"Alright, we will discover that soon. As for now, what is the last conscious thought you have as you take your last conscious breath?"

"*Pain.*"

I knew there was more work to do to release Karan's despair and sadness, so his pain need not be carried into another lifetime, such as Imogen's life now.

The spirit lifted out of Karan's body with that last thought, starting to feel lighter and brighter.

"I want to find her," said the spirit.

And in the light, the girl from the other village was waiting to greet Karan. She was still lovely with those unforgettable eyes. Karan's consciousness was awash with the many questions flowing through it. In the light, we simply allowed the spirits to unpack all the answers:

Why did you never show up?

They found out about us and killed me.

How did they kill you?

They hung me.

When?

That day.

Uncontrollable tears cascaded down Imogen's face. I suggested she could now release her fear of loneliness and let it roll away with the tears streaming down her face.

I softly spoke, "You know she cared, didn't she? She gave this relationship her life. With that love and care, you were never truly alone, were you?"

Imogen nodded her head in a silent response to my questions.

"Back in the forest, when you were waiting, did she come to the meeting point in spirit?"

"Yes, she did!" Imogen raised her voice, delighted. "She saw everything. She was there *with* me." More tears flowed down Imogen's already tear-streaked face.

"But perhaps you did not realize she was there because you were so focused on missing her."

I suggested that, in spirit, they meet up with each other at their special spot in the forest by the river. In that significant place and on the river's calm surface, the lovers watched six lifetimes reflected at them. Six lifetimes they had lived together: four romantic relationships, most of which ended up being torn apart in tragedy.

"What is the lesson in being torn apart?"

"We will always be together," Imogen replied without hesitation.

"That's weird." Judgingly, Imogen's analytical conscious voice spoke up.

"Always torn apart. Always *together*." I recognized it might not make sense to the linear and logical mind. But it made perfect sense to me as the regressionist who works daily in non-linear reality. I was about to share my thought with Imogen, but at that moment, I heard a voice within me saying: *This is her path, allow her the space to come to her own realizations.*

Each physical life is a story we tell. In these stories, we are torn apart. But we are the storytellers, and as storytellers, we are constantly weaving, co-writing our stories together.

Each physical life is a dream. In these dreams, we are torn apart. It is us who are the dreamers. In that identity, we are forever together.

Bringing the session to a close, I asked the spirits if they would meet again in this life. The answer was yes, that soul would find her again. All Imogen needed to do was continue living her life as she had been doing.

"She's been looking for me." This time around, there will be no reason to be torn apart. I asked Imogen if she had a question.

"Will I recognize you?" Imogen carried on her dialogue within herself.

The answer came confidently. "I will recognize you, and I will make sure you do it, too. Remove the pressure, and just go with the flow." It is going to be a cosmic date arranged from another lifetime. This time around, I knew both would show up.

In this never-ending expansion, healing is less about adding something to ourselves than finally letting go of the weight that no longer belongs to us.

One week after our session, I wrote Imogen-Karan's story. As promised, I emailed a draft to Imogen for correction and editing. Imogen's response came quickly; within half an hour, she wrote back with some exciting news:

> "… I met him two days after our session! He still has those unforgettably beautiful eyes. We are dating now, and I have never felt so happy! It's just been a week, but it feels like I have known him since forever. We just want to see each other all the time. It feels like we're inseparable. I cannot begin to explain the love we feel for each other.
>
> Thank you so much for getting me past my fear. If we are not torn apart in this life and get married, I will surely invite you to our wedding."
>
> Imogen

A Past Life Drama

What Goes Around

I do not have a television at home, but my life is certainly not lacking in drama. Doing past life regressions with clients sometimes feels like I am working on a blockbuster movie, complete with plot twists, action-adventure, big emotions, and surprise endings. Not unlike the movies, drama in a past life regression can be therapeutic, entertaining, and often both.

Phoebe's story was one of those cases. Curiosity brought the stunning beauty with dark, curly hair to my practice. Before booking an appointment with me, she had read many of my blog posts about my hypnotherapy work, the human mind, and consciousness. The young woman hoped to clear and heal her emotional blockages within relationships, learn more about life, and uncover her life purpose. She expressed her anger towards her family members; whenever her parents fought, she felt protective of her father yet did not feel comfortable sharing anything with him. Instead, Phoebe always felt a desire to escape him. Her feelings towards her mother were equally ambivalent, love and hate, anger, and sadness.

It was not until our second regression session that the Hollywood-esque drama arose— a classic tale of romance, love triangles, jealousy, and of course, murder.

In a trance, the small Phoebe sitting on my couch began to describe herself as a big, burly man named Robert. Well after dark in a 1930s bar, Robert stood stunned and panicked, looking down the business end of a gun. The man levelling the weapon at Robert's head squeezed the trigger.

It is not uncommon in a past life regression that the opening scene is also the moment of death. To find out more, I took Robert back to an earlier point in the evening: he and a group of men sat around a card table gambling. Even though he was winning, Robert felt stressed and anxious. One of his fellow gamblers, Melvin, had heatedly accused Robert of cheating at the game. In his mounting fury, Melvin bolted out of his chair, knocking the game's table over. Rushing the big man, he cornered him against the wall and drew his gun.

Robert stood stunned.

That was it.

Melvin's reaction seemed intense for just a simple card game. Needing more context, I moved Robert back in time: He was married and had a three-year-old daughter. Under the watchful eye of their big family dog, Robert's wife Sandra spent her days caring for their young daughter and tending to their large country home with its generous front and back yards. Every day, Robert went off to work in an office where he was an accountant. Melvin was there, too. He lived close by, the three of them having been friends since childhood. Tears crept silently down Phoebe's beautiful face when Melvin's name was mentioned.

"He slept with my wife," Robert said.

"How do you know?"

"I came home for lunch one afternoon and found them in bed."

"Go to that moment now. What do they do when you discover them in bed together?"

"They just look at me."

"Shocked?"

"Yes."

"What happened next?"

"I'm confused…." Robert paused for a long time.

"What did you do then?"

"I sat down on a chair."

"And what did they do?"

"They quickly got dressed. Said, 'Sorry. I'm so sorry.' But I can't feel any anger. I'm too sad to be angry. Why would they do that to me?"

"Are you sad because you have been betrayed by your wife? Or, because you were betrayed by your best friend?"

Robert hesitated before answering, "More, my best friend." He stopped momentarily before continuing, "I feel sick to my stomach."

Silently, I sat there with Robert and breathed with him a while before speaking again, "In a moment, you will start to feel better. What did you say to your wife?"

Now, Robert raised his voice, his anger bleeding into sadness, "Why did you do that to me?"

"What did she answer?"

"She's crying. She says, 'You are never here for me. You work all the time.'"

"Do you work too much? To the point that Sandra feels neglected, lonely?"

"Yes. But it is a man's responsibility to provide for his family! I have to work a lot. For my family!"

The look on Robert-Phoebe's face was one of utter confusion. It was not that he loved his work so much; he loved his family more. For Robert, working those long hours was an expression of his love and duty; he worked long and hard to make more money, to provide all that he perceived his family needed to be happy, healthy, and well.

Interestingly, one of Phoebe's relationship complaints was that her four-year, on-again-off-again boyfriend was too focused on his work and career, leaving Phoebe feeling like he had little time for her.

"What about Melvin? What does he do? He doesn't have to work as much?"

"He's a business owner."

"Has your wife ever complained about it before that you work too much?"

"No!"

"Ask her why she hadn't brought up this issue with you?"

"She says, 'You wouldn't have listened. You wouldn't have changed anything.'"

"*Would* you have listened and changed had she brought it up?"

"No. The money is important."

"Okay. What are you going to do now?"

"I don't know," Robert's voice faltered. "I guess I'll pretend like it didn't happen."

"Because…"

"I can't imagine not having my family. What's the point if I don't have any family?"

"What about your friendship with Melvin? Are you going to pretend he's still a friend?"

"There's tension there. And anger."

"You towards him or him towards you?"

"Both."

"Why would he be angry with you?"

"I just don't know."

A year after Robert caught his wife and best friend together, Melvin walked into the bar where Robert was playing and joined the game. The silent anger between the two friends took a firm seat at the table alongside the other gamblers. But luck was on Robert's side that evening; hand after hand, he kept winning. Until Melvin, unable to muzzle his anger any longer, called Robert out for cheating and accused him of stealing Sandra away. "You know you never made her happy," Melvin shouted at his friend.

"How do you feel when you hear that?" I asked Robert.

"I'm confused. I tried so hard to make her happy."

"It sounds like he cares a lot about Sandra."

"Yeah."

"Many years ago, did Sandra have to choose between you and Melvin?"

"No. Sandra and I were together. Melvin never said anything."

"So, you never knew that Melvin loved Sandra back then?"

"No."

"Then how could it be that you stole Sandra from him?"

"I don't know. That's what he said to me. He said, 'You never cared for her.' Of course, I cared for her! She's my wife, my entire life. I worked so hard for her."

"Could he mean you never spent enough time with her?"

"Melvin said I was never there for her when she needed me. He asked me what else did I expect? But I *do* care for her. I'm heartbroken."

"Maybe not the way she wanted to be cared for?"

Robert went silent.

With the handgun pointing at Robert's head, moments before Melvin pulled the trigger, I asked Robert what his last thought was. "'She's all yours,'" was his mournful reply.

"Gently, easily, pull yourself out of your body. Feeling light, feeling bright and free. You are out of your body now.

Hovering over it before you move on. What do you see?" Robert's spirit relayed what it was watching mechanically.

"Melvin is sitting. By the body. He looks sad."

"Allow yourself to know how the story ended after you passed on."

"Melvin and Sandra get together. I see them hugging each other."

"Is Sandra happy about that?"

"No. She is sad."

"And your daughter? What happens to her?"

Robert took a long, melancholic pause before speaking. "She shuts down, clams up. She doesn't like Melvin and misses her father."

"Do you still feel anger and sadness now?"

"Yes."

I guided Robert to release those emotions. Robert confided that he visited Sandra's dreams from time to time, where he told her again and again how much he cared for her. Robert's interpretation of caring for his wife had been to provide his family with all the creature comforts money could buy: a big house with big yards. Yet, Sandra's need was to have and spend more time together.

"If you were to visit Melvin in his dreams, what might you say to him? Once upon a time, he was your best friend."

Robert took another long pause before he finally spoke. "I want to thank him for being there for Sandra. For not leaving her to be lonely. But it was not fair."

"It was not fair because…"

"Because now he's saying he loved her forever, and I never knew that."

"Why didn't he express his love towards Sandra before?"

"Sandra wouldn't respond to him, and he believed she loved me. It was out of respect for her choice that he didn't say anything sooner."

Melvin had always loved Sandra and had respectfully bowed out, allowing her to marry Robert. But love is long, and Melvin never stopped loving Sandra. Robert's steadfast ambition of making ever more money only created a divide in his marriage. A space that Melvin stepped in to fill. With that knowledge, Robert's spirit agreed to move on.

As my session with Phoebe came to a close, she recognized souls from Robert's life present in her current life: her maternal grandmother was indeed Sandra, Robert's wife; her mother, whom she loved, hated, and felt anger and sadness towards was Melvin. In comparison, Robert's daughter was Phoebe's best friend, Sheila. Phoebe's father, however, was not identified in the life of Robert. It was in our later sessions that Phoebe's deep, intensely charged emotions towards her father came to light.

I could not help but notice the relationship similarities between lives. As a woman in this life, Phoebe had the same issues with her boyfriend as Robert's wife had had with him. A partner who spent all his time working instead of spending time with her. A partner whose rationale for working long hours was that he needed to build a solid financial foundation for them both. I could not help but wonder, was this karma? Or something else...?

Friend of My Father's

A Soul's Recycling

I grew up in China, and I still have memories of the Sino-Vietnamese War, referred to as the "Defensive Counterattack Against Vietnam." I was a young girl at the time, and even though it was a short-lived war[2], it was a major and brutal conflict. Every day, my family listened to the radio for news about the war.

With time, the collective memory of the war went into a file marked 'Forgiving.' As a young woman, I visited Vietnam three times. Despite the beautiful countryside and the impression of peace, I could still feel the memories that weighed heavily on that land.

Eileen was a 26-year-old Chinese-Vietnamese woman born and raised in Oregon state. Vacationing in Vancouver, British Columbia, for a few days, Eileen had decided to do some spiritual travel as well and booked a PLR session with me. She arrived at her session well prepared to explore, and presented me with a piece of paper with four, neatly written bullet points:

- Why do I have this greyish blue birthmark on my right palm?
- Why do I have a troubled relationship with my family, especially with my father?
- What is my life purpose?

---

[2] The Sino-Vietnamese border war's official duration was only a single month from February to March in 1979. However, the armed conflict that followed lasted for ten years.

- What is the cause of my drug and smoking addictions?

Discussing these points further, Eileen shared that she had seen a psychic a year earlier and was told the birthmark on her palm was from a past life war. She continued to explain that her troubled relationship with her father was essentially caused by her lack of trust, a distrust that fanned out to include her entire family. "I don't know why. I can't help it," the young woman exclaimed with a puzzled look.

While she liked teaching and working with children, Eileen felt there was more she could be doing with her life. "Such as what?" I asked.

"Like massage therapy or something. I'm drawn to healing."

"What stops you from going for it then?"

"I'm not sure if it's the right path for me. Teaching seems to be more stable work."

For someone's first hypnotherapy session, I often use a finger spreading induction[3] and decided to do one with Eileen. I had Eileen place her hand in front of her eyes, with her eyes gazing at the tip of her middle finger. Her attention fully absorbed, I suggested that her fingers would gently and subtly separate. This induction would create greater ease in bypassing Eileen's conscious and analytical mind, allowing more unrestricted access to her deep subconscious memories.

With Eileen, this induction was an even more meaningful exercise. I planned to have Eileen gaze at her right hand, spread her fingers, go into hypnosis, and let her right hand,

---

[3] You can learn more about finger spreading inductions by watching my tutorial video, Hypnosis Finger Spreading Induction Demonstration on my Kemila Zsange YouTube channel.

with its greyish-blue birthmark, start to tell the story of a past life. Eileen proved herself to be an excellent hypnosis subject. She dropped quickly and easily into a deep hypnotic state simply by me explaining to her that this would happen without her needing to raise her hand and spread her fingers.

A forest scene came for Eileen, one she had dreamt many times before in her younger years: she and a friend were running for their lives, attempting to flee the horrors of war.

"You are running in the forest with your friend," I repeated. Repetition is a technique hypnotherapists use called hypnosis revivification[4].

"It's like a village forest," Eileen corrected.

I was unsure if I understood what she meant by "village forest," but I decided to use it as it sounded, rather than simply assuming she had meant a village *in* a forest.

"Yes. A village forest. Is it a good friend you are fleeing with?"

"Yeah. I hope so." Interesting answer. I considered my next question, but Eileen spoke again, "I can't move further beyond this scene."

"That is all right. This is a familiar scene because you have dreamt it many times in the past. But the running cannot happen without the story. Simply allow yourself to drop into the forest. You will *know*."

---

[4] Revivification is a therapeutic technique where the therapist echoes or repeats a client's answers back to them. This helps solicit additional details about an experience and is a key component of successful hypnotic regression. The more details a hypnotherapist asks for, the more of the client's senses are engaged, and the more anchored into the experience the client becomes. In addition to producing a deeper hypnotic state, revivification facilitates more intense memory recall. In a sense, clients virtually relive their past life experiences.

"My father told me he lost a friend in the war." I realized this was now Eileen's conscious mind speaking. "There was a time when I wanted to join the army. But my father was against the idea and urged me not to do it. He told me then how he lost a childhood friend in the war, although he never told me the circumstances. Ever since then, I have dreamt this scene. Maybe I took what my father told me and imagined this scene?"

It is expected that when things come up in regression, the analytical mind wishes to rationalize them. Sitting with Eileen, I could easily perceive the thoughts flowing through her mind: *I wanted to join the army. Father didn't want me to. He told me about losing a friend in the war. Then I started having recurring dreams, as my mind began to imagine how my father lost his friend. Now my so-called past life regression is just the awakening of that old dream, something my imagination created based on my father's old story.* As a hypnotherapist, I know that *everything* happens for a reason.

"Just allow yourself to go deeper into the scene now," I instructed softly. "It is a familiar scene, but you can go deeper into it and explore more details this time. Allow the story to continue from there. You are running…"

"I can't go further. It stops."

"But the story itself does not stop, does it? You are running…" I told myself to be patient. "Other soldiers are chasing you?" I took it for granted that Eileen and her friend were trying to evade soldiers in the war.

"No. I'm not a soldier." Eileen responded quickly. Despite her belief that she could not access more information, Eileen did seem to know more than what she previously believed. "I'm more a villager."

"That's right. You are a villager. Are you a male or a female?"

"Male." Eileen's answer was firm and immediate.

"That's right. If you know the answer, do you eventually make it to safety? Do you escape?"

Eileen whispered meekly, "I was caught."

"You were caught. Both of you?"

"No. Just me." Eileen's tone changed, and the voice of her conscious mind again came through, "I just seem to be stuck on this single scene."

"And you think you imagined this scene based on your father's old story? Is that right?"

"Yes."

I had decided to hijack the rationale of Eileen's conscious mind: "Well, if you can imagine this scene, you can easily imagine the rest of the story and also the beginning of the story. Every story has a beginning and an end. You can freely move backward and forward. You cannot be stuck since this scene is imagined anyway."

"Okay. From knowing what my dad told me before, it's during the Chinese-Vietnamese war. I feel like I am a Chinese person living in Vietnam, and the Vietnamese do not want us there. That is why we are running."

"Those behind you, are they armed?"

"I can't say for sure." Suddenly, Eileen became very upset and started sobbing. So, I guided her to rise above the scene and tell me what she saw from that more neutral perspective.

"The first thing that came to mind was being stabbed."

"Stabbed. Where?"

"In my hand! Maybe it was because I was trying to run, and they grabbed my hand. The hand feels very warm."

"As the warmth in your hand comes to your awareness, allow yourself to know: Do you know those people?"

"No, I don't," she cried plaintively. "They don't know us either. They just identified us as being Chinese and started chasing us."

"What happened next?"

"I don't know! I can't remember. My hand is burning. That's all," the young lady sobbed.

"What of your friend?"

"It seems he got away. But they caught me."

"What did they do with you?"

"They left me there."

"They left you there with your hand burning. Can you move?"

Eileen then came out of hypnosis, saying she needed to use the restroom. I gave her a suggestion to re-enter hypnosis before I guided her to leave the past life scene and return to the present. Eileen opened her eyes, got up, used the washroom, and returned to lay back down on the couch.

"I don't think I have any more information."

"That's right. You don't 'think' you have more information because the mind thinks, and the body *knows*. Only your body can have more information, more memories. Your thinking mind doesn't know, does it? If it did, you would not need to be here with me, would you?"

The session had started well but no longer flowed smoothly. The traumatic event in Eileen's past life posed a challenge, and her conscious, analytical mind kept rationalizing the memories. Yet, despite all her overanalyzing, she could draw out more information, bit by tiny bit, eliciting more emotions.

It is not uncommon when a client breaks away from their hypnotic trance to drop even deeper into it once they go back in. We call this fractionation. I intended to guide Eileen back into the scene of that doubted past life. I also anticipated she would recall more information when I did.

"I'm just a kid," she began.

"How old are you?"

"Maybe twelve."

"Your friend, is he the same age?"

"Yes. And those other people too. The ones who chased us are also kids."

"Do you know them?"

"No. My friend and I were just walking when the other kids spotted us and began chasing us. There were more of them, we were outnumbered, and I ended up getting caught."

"How long did you stay there where you got caught?"

"Two hours. I don't know what happened to my friend. I don't know if he was eventually caught, too. I waited for him, though. I didn't want to get lost even more. But maybe he didn't care. Maybe he ran away." Tears rolled down Eileen's face.

"How do you feel at this point?"

"Betrayed. I waited for him, but he never came back."

There must have been more going on with the young boy than just a wounded hand because next, he was dying, and his dying thought was, "I am alone."

I did not have the opportunity to ask all the questions I was thinking of at that moment: Perhaps, the boy was not merely "waiting" for his friend to return but savagely wounded and bleeding to death during that time? The pain from his hand simply masked the seriousness of his fatal wounds. Or could it be that the physical agony and emotional pain of that trauma were too great for Eileen to express such details? Whatever was missing from the boy's recounting of events, the act of dying opened another floodgate of tears for Eileen.

As the spirit drifted away from the body, he learned that his friend had escaped. The other boy had kept running, eventually finding refuge in a different place where he began a new life for himself. It was unclear if the boy knew of his friend's capture. He may not have had time to look back while running for his own life.

I asked the spirit, "That friend, is this person present, in any way, shape or form, in this life of Eileen's?"

"I don't know. I don't *want* to know! I feel…" The boy's spirit paused as if gathering its thoughts, "…not angry. I am resentful and mad. I don't even know if he knew what happened to me, that I died. I don't feel appreciated."

"This feeling of betrayal and resentment holds the key to trust and trusting. Which means as long as you hold on to these feelings, this grudge, you won't trust. Do you understand?"

"Yeah."

The spirit speaking as Eileen shared with me how every time there were news reports of school shootings, Eileen had the impulse to go and save the innocent children. Even if that meant she had to take the bullets herself.

"Could it be that since you were captured, they let your friend go? In that sense, did you not save your friend's life? You died to save him."

I noticed that Eileen had dropped deep into thought as if an inner shift were occurring. "Yesss," was her only reply.

Guiding the discarnate soul to the light, the soul met Will, its spirit guide. Will told us that all that had occurred was meant to be; the boy was meant to die saving his friend's life. That forgiveness was to be the lesson in that lifetime, and once Eileen learned to forgive, she could move forward on her path as a healer.

I looked at the sheet of questions Eileen had brought to the session and asked Will, "What is the significance of Eileen having a birthmark on her right palm?"

Will's answer was clear and direct, "Like many marks, it is to remember. In this life and in Eileen's case, the birthmark on her hand serves double duty. It is to remember both forgiveness and the healing ability she holds in her hands. She has had many other lifetimes practicing healing, but she needed to learn forgiveness. The short life in Vietnam was the start of a brief lesson on forgiveness. Eileen has chosen her father as the person she needs to forgive in this life."

It was like a powerful floodlight, rather than a lightbulb, that went off in my head when I heard that. I was dumbfounded by clarity. At that moment, everything made perfect sense. Eileen's father *was* that friend who escaped, and Eileen's past life was as her father's childhood friend who died in the war! Discouraging his daughter from becoming a soldier was her father's way of honouring and appreciating his friend's sacrifice. Perhaps, there was more depth to her father's inner awareness than merely losing a friend in the war?

Will continued his revelatory guidance: Eileen smoked and used drugs to mask her suffering, attempting to escape her physical pain and the sting of betrayal associated with her death as that young boy. *Remembering* was part of Eileen's healing journey. As she fully remembered, she would be able to release her resentment and no longer suffer through her physical pain. With nothing left to mask, Eileen would be able to free herself of cigarettes and drugs.

I thanked Will and was about to bring the session to a close. But I wanted to take advantage of what we had learned from her guide and that past life. I instructed Eileen to go across space and time, back to that lost boy who had died saving his friend, and just comfort him as a healer might do.

Eileen came out of hypnosis, only partially remembering what happened during the regression. I explained to her that her father's recall of losing a childhood friend in the war, and her recurring dream of it, were, in fact, a shared memory across lifetimes. For a long time, Eileen was speechless. Then, once again, the tears silently ran down her face, this time, shedding tears of forgiveness and release.

One Hour, Seven Lifetimes

Even "Darkness" Seeks Light

Emily booked her follow-up hypnotherapy appointment by email. While her emails were always short and to the point, now, sitting in my office, she could go on at length, using a lot of words to describe her emotional turmoil. She launched into her list of things she desired to let go of: fear, doubt, judgments, ego, and anything else that was causing her intense abdominal physical reactions. Her visceral reactions prevented Emily from living her life to its fullest: "I know I unconsciously hide things that are holding me down…"

If you know you unconsciously hide things, you can no longer call it 'unconscious.' It has already been brought to your conscious awareness, I thought, but I let Emily continue.

The young woman constantly read self-help books and worked on her self-worth, yet she still relapsed into suffocating thoughts and fears.

Seeking a therapist for some time, Emily said she was attracted by the spiritual aspect of what I do: "the fact that it's deeper than just words."

So, here we were, a staggeringly beautiful young actress consumed with feelings of fear, anxiety, stress, and unworthiness. Any of Emily's presenting issues could be the entry point for hypnosis. While I was contemplating the best approach for making this a productive session, I caught Emily saying, "I just feel as if there are two parts of me inside: the good part, which wants to grow and loves reading Wayne Dyer's books, and the evil part of me…" Something clicked for me. Emily was not only presenting me with issues; she was also offering pathways to solutions. I had Emily make herself comfortable. Using my quickest three-word hypnosis induction, I commanded, "Close your eyes!"

In a more soothing tone, I added, "Just like your morning meditation, gently go there, to that place of peace and tranquility."

It only took a couple of minutes for Emily to go deep into hypnosis. From that state, I invited the part of her called "Evil" to come out and speak with me because here in my office, it was safe, and it was welcome. Emily's breathing had started coming rapidly, and her facial muscles had shifted entirely. Now sobbing, Emily wore the face of a frightened child.

"I— Am— Scared," she whispered in a young boy's voice, struggling to articulate each word.

"What are you scared of?"

"People. I'm scared they don't love me."

"What's your name?"

"B-Ber-Bernie." Still having difficulty speaking, Emily-Bernie's voice trembled.

"Bernie, how old are you?"

"Thirteen."

"You are thirteen."

I had not intended to have a past life regression session with Emily but a traditional Parts Therapy[5] one instead. And I was not at all sure what was going on, so I asked, "Bernie, what year is this for you?"

---

[5] Parts Therapy is a therapeutic technique intended to address the blocks that can arise when different parts of a patient, e.g., ego, inner child, identity, psyche, needs, and desires are actively competing and/or conflicting with one another.

"1232," came Bernie's stilted reply.

Quite possibly, Bernie was simply a past life personality of Emily's. Equally possible, it could be a case of spirit attachment. Curious, I asked Bernie why he was afraid that people did not love him. He described how his younger brother was the family favourite, leaving him feeling bitter, isolated, and unlikeable.

I wanted Bernie to tell his story, "Bernie, what happened when you were 13?"

"Oh!" He seemed genuinely surprised by my question. He took some time to ponder it as if recalling a long-forgotten memory. When Bernie finally answered, he spoke in a halting voice, "I think. I was. Drowned."

As Bernie's memory gradually returned, he could share his story with me: a stranger had drowned him in a well on his family's farm. After dying in the wet and dark, Bernie had felt anger, horror, and fear of no longer having a physical form.

"So, what did you do?"

"I went to my baby sister."

"How old was she at the time?"

"Two."

"What was her name?"

"Elisabeth."

"Why did you choose to go to your baby sister?"

"She always has so many angels around her. I like to be around angels too," Emily-Bernie smiled.

"So, you just went to her and attached to her?"

"Yes."

"Did Elisabeth know this?"

"Yes. I think she did. But she didn't mind."

On a hunch, I asked, "And your baby sister, Elisabeth is Emily in this life?" I recalled Emily saying that anything angelic always drew her attention.

"Yes," Bernie confirmed.

"Now tell me, Bernie, how many lifetimes since attaching to Elisabeth have you been with this soul on Earth?"

The answer came quick and sure, "Seven."

"Seven lifetimes." I was a little taken aback and needed to gather my thoughts, "So, what do you do? When the body dies, you just hang out here until the soul is incarnated into another body?"

"Yes."

"Tell me, Bernie, about the seven lifetimes…"

"Once she was Tommy." Bernie interrupted me mid-question. He happily volunteered the information as though he found it amusing, "That was fun! Tommy lived in California and partied a lot. He was heavy into drugs. He died too young, though. Only 21."

"Overdose?"

"Yes, but that was a fun life."

"Were you involved in Tommy's drug use, Bernie?"

"Umm? Maybe? I was just scared. I didn't know what to do!" Bernie's reaction raised my suspicions. It was a little too defensive and sounded a lot like the excuse of a mischief-maker. After seven lifetimes attached to his sister's soul, Bernie was still exploiting his fear to justify his behaviour. His emotion *was* real, but mischievousness can mask underlying fear.

"Bernie, look at the seven lifetimes. Can you clearly see how much confusion you have caused this soul who was once your baby sister?" As Bernie reviewed his seven lifetimes attached to the Elisabeth-Tommy-Emily soul, Emily's eyes raced behind her closed lids.

"Yes, look! Look clearly at how much trouble this being who once was your baby sister has lived and experienced. Lifetime after lifetime, because of *your* fear."

"I didn't know! What can I do?" But Bernie's outcry seemed to spark his own insights before I could offer him any. "Maybe, I can be born one more time? I want to be reborn into a new, different life!"

"Yes, Bernie! It all started with you being afraid of not having a body, remember? But you know, the best way to have a body is to be born again!"

"Oh!" Bernie cried excitedly, "Maybe I can be born as a dog? Can I come back as a dog?"

"Why not? You know we all love dogs. But this you have to discuss with…" I did not know what word to use here, "…whoever is in charge after you leave."

"Oh…" Bernie pondered this.

"Now, Bernie, would you like to leave Elisabeth?"

"Yes…" his voice trailed off.

"Good." I responded encouragingly, "Look around then, maybe upwards? What do you see?"

"I see light."

"How do you feel?"

"I feel *good*."

"Good, Bernie. The light is coming for *you*. You said you feel good, that you like to be around angels. The lights *are* angels. Now allow the light to come closer to you. Do you feel peace?"

Bernie nodded.

"Warmth?"

Another nod.

"Will you go now with the light?"

A final nod.

"Before you go, may I ask a favour of you? Could you please scan Emily's body? Look for any areas that are dark or grey?" It's common practice in Spirit Release Therapy to ask the cooperating entity to help check for anything else, which could be emotional baggage or other entities yet discovered.

"There's this grey stuff in her stomach, on the right."

"What is it?"

"I'm not sure."

Remembering Emily mentioned her intense emotional-visceral reactions in her stomach, I asked, "Could you please take it to the light with you?"

"Yes, I can do that."

On his way to the light, Bernie shared one more insight: Emily's soulmates, including her mother, boyfriend, and best friend, formed a diamond shape in the young lady's life. I could sense Bernie looked calm and peaceful now, almost glowing. I knew he was now ready to go.

"Thank you, Bernie, very much for your help."

"Thank YOU! Thank you... Thank you..." The voice drifted off, moving further and further away.

"Thank you, Bernie. Good-bye! May you be reborn as a dog!" I almost chuckled at this genuine wish.

"Goodbye," Bernie giggled cheerfully.

Incredibly, with its soul attachment, past lives, and life-between-lives experiences, the whole session had only taken us an hour. I emerged Emily from the regression, and once again, the woman lying on my couch looked like Emily. She opened her eyes, wide and bright, tears remaining on her beautifully glowing face.

Before leaving my office, the slender actress turned towards me, revealing a mixture of surprise, gratitude, and relief and said, "I feel like I've just shed 30 pounds of dead weight!" Indeed, she had done just that, shedding a soul that had been with her for so many, many lifetimes.

Left sitting alone, I could not believe how easy it was. One hour of work: release from seven lifetimes of emotional pain and discomfort! I was amazed. I had done some type of hypnosis or trance work in previous lifetimes, and I wondered about what 'might have been.' Had I known Emily in one of my past lives, I might have released Bernie's soul attachment to her long ago, saving her from countless heartache endured over numerous lifetimes. I continued to ponder time, different approaches I might have employed, and all other possibilities available to me, a space-time travelling hypnotherapist. Could I have first regressed Emily back to her life as Elisabeth and released Bernie's soul back then? Much like time travelling, sci-fi movies where a character travels back in time to kill the killer before the killer commits the crime. But was there even such a thing as linear time? I felt so much love and appreciation towards Emily, the Light that came for Bernie, and Bernie himself.

Boundless Love

The Stories We Choose

Karen had first contacted me from out of town, voicing her interest in having a past life regression session. She was curious about using hypnosis to access past life information but had some concerns about the process: could everyone even be hypnotized? At her high school graduation, a hypnotist had been invited to the ceremony but could not put her "under."

Our consultation seemed to address Karen's questions and concerns satisfactorily. She then conveyed another concern, that she was hesitant about using Skype for such a session and asked whether I had any travel plans. Unfortunately, I did not plan to revisit Ireland any time soon. We brought our consultation to a close, with Karen advising she would need to take some time to think about booking a PLR session in the future.

The future turned out to be nine months later. Karen again reached out with some misgivings. However, nine months appeared to have been enough time for the 25-year-old to consider things and come to a decision.

Karen began our video session by professing she did not have any real issues; she was simply interested in past lives. I proposed she could leave the session wide open to see what would come up. Or, to help me better guide her through the process, she could give me a direction.

"Maybe relationships then. I seem to make good friends with men. I've dated several, but I can't seem to commit," she reflected.

"What happens when it comes to commitment?"

"I always find something wrong with them."

That was all the direction I needed to start us off. From my iPad, I watched Karen slide into a past life.

Dusk was settling around the small room where Inge lay in bed. Through the window, in the glimmering twilight, the girl could just make out the silhouettes of pine trees clinging to the Swiss slopes.

"It sounds very pretty," I commented.

"I guess," she replied, "but it's what I've seen every day my whole life. It's nothing special."

It was 1907, Switzerland, and a 12-year-old Inge lived in a small mountain cabin with her parents and three older brothers. With the help of his sons, her father supported his family by logging the surrounding mountain forests. Because Inge was so young, small, and a girl, she was no help to her father's work.

"Girls are useless," her father would say. Over time, her eldest brother would also adopt the same derisive view as his father. Leaving the young Inge feeling comfortable only with her mother and two other brothers. A deep wound had already formed, though. Inge harboured the belief that her father could never like her because she was born a girl. Thus, began Inge's troubled life in Switzerland at the turn of the twentieth century.

In a mountain valley was a town. It was a picturesque town in the way of small Swiss towns, where locals from all around sold goods they had grown or crafted; bought the things they needed; participated in or attended town activities and socials. The town was also the home to Inge's school, and on school days, the small girl would pick her way down the mountain to attend lessons. In time, Inge became best friends with a classmate named Jakob. Inge and Jakob did as much together as time allowed; helping each other with their schoolwork, playing together after school, joking around, and generally having fun as only children can.

Their friendship blossomed into adolescent affection, and affection gave way to romance as they emerged into adulthood. When Inge turned twenty, she married Jakob and moved off the mountainside to live with Jakob in the town. Shortly after their wedding, Jakob began working in the local government and, in little time, assumed additional responsibilities in his field. "He is in charge of people," Inge stated proudly. Her husband was the mirror opposite of his father-in-law: Jakob was kind and compassionate; creative and industrious; funny and intelligent. He possessed a natural ease with people and quickly gained the respect of everyone he met.

The young couple started a family, with Inge giving birth to four children in quick succession: two boys and two girls. They were happy and content in their lives. Jakob soon rose to a senior position at work, and Inge was a happy mother raising her children. After making it through the war years seemingly unscathed and surviving the subsequent Spanish Flu of 1918-1919, misfortune finally struck the happy family. It was early 1924, and Jakob and Inge's eldest son lay stricken with pneumonia. At first, the eight-year-old appeared only to have a mild cold. In a few days, though, his condition had worsened. The boy's health declined quickly after, and he died a week later.

The war years were harsh and unforgiving for the Swiss people; with food scarcity and rising grocery prices, there were also food rationings. The men were required to serve in the military, protecting the borders and Swiss independence. They received little pay and no compensation for the wages they had lost from their previous work. As fate would have it, Jakob's senior position in government exempted him from serving on the frontlines. Not only did he and his family avoid the struggle and the restrictions of war, but they prospered. Yet, success can breed envy, and envy, resentment. In turn, resentment often begets heartless action.

Shortly after the death of their son, the rumours began. Inge was the first to hear them: "Why should we trust someone to help us when they can't take care of their own child?" their neighbours and townsfolk asked. The family tried to ignore the rumours, but they only grew and morphed into uglier accusations: the boy lost his life because his parents were too preoccupied with their vanities and had failed to act quickly.

The death of their son had thrown the entire family into a deep and abiding sadness. Whether it was rumour solidifying into misguided belief, or a political move to deflect post-war public anger towards the government, Jakob was soon fired from his job, further devastating the already grieving family. He eventually found new work in a butcher's shop. It was dirty, unpleasant work. Jakob never liked it, and his wages were far less than he'd earned in his government job. With the loss of status and a comfortable livelihood, the couple decided to sell their home and start over in a bigger city.

The move to a new city was successful. Jakob secured a good position in a local office, and the family had found a comfortable home with a large veranda. Inge quickly made friends with the nearby housewives, inviting them over for afternoon tea on the large, wooden deck.

I guided Inge forward in time to the next significant event in her life. The year was 1937. Inge was forty-two and had just learned that her husband was having an affair. Adding insult to injury, Inge discovered that the affair had been going on long enough for her husband to sire a child with his mistress. Inge was devastated. Her husband, her oldest friend, had betrayed her. Shocked, mortified and deeply hurt, Inge and Jakob argued.

"You don't love me anymore."

"I do! I do love you! I do."

"I don't believe you!" Inge cried. "You wouldn't hurt me like this if you loved me. You are just like my father, hurting me."

Inge through Karen sobbed on the screen of my iPad.

"I thought he truly loved me. I must be a bad wife."

Jakob kept trying to plead and explain his actions to his wife, and a heartbroken Inge kept breaking down in tears, refusing to listen. The marriage was at an impasse, with both partners feeling hurt, undervalued, and unheard. Jakob eventually moved out, moving in with his mistress. For a while, Jakob and Inge remained living separately in the same city until he and his new family finally moved away.

Inge declined. Feeling abandoned, isolated, and alone, she lay in bed most days, having lost the will to get up. One of her daughters dutifully saw to her mother's basic needs and care. Although he often wrote, remaining in his children's lives through regular letters, they never saw Jakob again.

Over the next twenty years, the depression and loneliness never left Inge's side. At sixty-three years of age and on her deathbed, she still harboured a bitter resentment. Before moving on, I asked her spirit if it wished to visit anywhere. The soul answered yes, it would like to see how Jakob was doing.

"Now, without a body, you can go anywhere and everywhere you want to go. Just a thought of someone can take you to them." I counted down from three to one and said, "Find Jakob now. Where is he?"

"He is in a house sitting by a table."

"By himself? Or with someone?"

"With that woman and their now-grown child."

"How is Jakob doing?"

"He seems content, but there is also a heaviness about him. I sense a feeling of regret tinged with sadness."

I asked the spirit to access Jakob's thoughts and emotions towards Inge: "He still loves Inge and thinks about her often. He wishes he could have spent the rest of his life with her and regrets that he could not." Again, Karen began to cry.

From "being Jakob," Karen accessed even more information: "When Jakob and Inge first moved to the city, that woman used to work next door to his office. Jakob admired her because she was out in the world working. Where he was from, women did not work outside the home. Instead, they stayed home, tending to the house and children. Jakob was attracted to that difference. He had never intended to have a committed relationship with her. Then she became pregnant, and he had to do the responsible thing. He felt he had to help support her and their child."

"Do you still love him?"

"I always loved him."

"Do you now believe that Jakob always *did* love Inge?"

"I do." More tears crept down Karen's face.

"So, knowing that, would you forgive him?"

"No! Never!" The spirit was vehement in its rejection.

"What do you think about that woman?"

"She is doing her best to please him."

"How do you feel about her now?"

"Hatred."

"Can anything happen for you to forgive them?"

"Nothing can happen for me to forgive them." Same as when Inge was alive, nothing Jakob said or did would shift how she felt.

I guided the spirit to move on from that scene. It came upon its young-looking spirit guide, Paul. Paul escorted Inge's spirit to a gathering of five elders for a life review. The Elders acknowledged Inge's was a hard life. She had done her best, accomplishing what she had set out for her life plan. Yet, she needed to let go of her anger, hurt, and hate.

The soul had a tough time letting go, though. It understood forgiveness was needed on its path of growth, but on an action level, it lacked true motivation or clarity. I brought my attention back to Karen and asked her to compare her life and the life of Inge to observe if any parallels were present. Karen realized where her distrust and commitment phobia stemmed from and, under further observation, recognized some of the same souls in her own life as in Inge's, including some of Inge's family members.

It can be exceedingly tricky to let go when we are so much a part of our story, and when we are in love with the stories we have created. It is akin to being immersed in an illusion and not being conscious of how the illusion works. Love, however, has no boundaries; love simply loves. Love does not hurt. It is our ideas of love that cause pain. True love is limitless; it flows; it holds no singular form or state of being. It has no bounds. Love allows. It allows you to be who you are, to express who you are, in any way that you want. Love does not limit, control, or restrict. Love is the most genuine freedom of the soul.

Sometimes, in the name of love, we fall deeply enamoured with our own story, causing us great suffering. The way forward is to release ourselves from the story, embracing total acceptance of what was and is, knowing we are the powerful creators of our stories. Taking both comfort and full responsibility for each moment that we are constantly and consistently creating.

Rather than attempting to force the soul of Karen-Inge into forgiveness, I offered her an alternative. Instead of putting so much energy into bullying a story to work, she need not forgive anybody in this or other lifetimes. And when she chose to, she could finally set herself free.

Even though we may pray to God or the angels, our prayers are not always answered in the way we might expect. And if we are aware, we will see we *always* get what we have co-created. We can spend our time rationalizing what is right, wrong, just, and fair, but it does not make it true. In tailoring our rationalizations to fit the feelings we have attached to our stories, we only amplify the intensity of our stories. In that soulful state and with the help of her guide and guiding Elders, the soul came to know that one lifetime is but one story in the eternal library of the soul.

Karen had a choice: she could continue to make her stories "fit" and keep repeating her cycles of incarnation on Earth. Or she could surrender and let love be. The shift I felt in Karen said she had chosen the latter.

Coming out of hypnosis, Karen opened her eyes and said, "Wow, this works! Even with the time difference and us being on Skype, I felt your presence right there by my side. It's amazing!"

Thinking it had taken Karen nine months to be ready for this, I smiled and asked, "Do you remember everything?"

"I do." Karen reflected for a moment. "But I can feel it already fading like a dream."

"That's fine." I said, "The story may fade, but the lessons will not. Love does not fade. It is always fresh and new. Can you allow yourself to love again? That is a question Inge would likely have for you in this life. Can you *trust* love? Can you embrace love fully again? Do you need to protect yourself from love? I will leave you with those questions to ponder. You don't need to come up with any answers right now. Just ponder these questions for the next little while."

Karen nodded her head wordlessly. I had sensed a shift; I could tell the session had served as an opening for her to start allowing herself to be her whole, authentic self.

So many external sources tell women that their identification as a woman is bound to being part of a romantic relationship. In this lifetime, Karen has the freedom to love whomever she chooses rather than find someone who loves her. I knew our work had been to bring this freedom and empowerment into her awareness.

A Secret Beach

When in Doubt, Choose Love

Tomoko was getting ready to head out after our appointment, and I seized the opportunity to get her consent: "You have read my blog, so you know that I sometimes write about my cases. I feel your story is worth sharing. Do I have your permission to write about your story? There won't be--" I meant to say, "There won't be any identifiable information," but Tomoko didn't let me finish.

"Yes, yes! Yes, of course. You can write anything about it. Actually, I will write about it myself!" I was first impressed by this level of eagerness before even meeting Tomoko. She had booked her past life regression session online and, in the Note section, had written: "This is my very first time doing Past Life Regression. I am both excited and nervous!"

Excitement and nervousness are the same neutral energy, just filtered through different belief systems to be experienced on the lighter side as excitement or the denser side as nervousness and anxiety. I work very well with that energy. So, it was not an understatement to say that I was looking forward to meeting with Tomoko.

Tomoko, a young Japanese woman sporting a trendy hairstyle, showed up to our appointment, bringing that warmth and eagerness with her. Her hair was a vivid expression of her liveliness: some sections long, short, and shaved, some sections dyed azure blue, canary yellow, and cotton candy pink.

The thirty-one-year-old explained that through her regression experience, she intended to explore why it was so difficult for her to open up in relationships: "It all starts very well. I meet people easily." Then, looking a little more serious, she added, "By the way, I'm bi-sexual, so I date both men and women." After seeing me nod my head encouragingly, she continued, "It's always great at the beginning when everything is casual. But when things get more intimate, when it's time to open up and be vulnerable, I just shut them out. I give them the cold shoulder."

"So, that is a pattern you have noticed?"

"Yes, it's a pattern."

"Different people, different genders, the same result?"

"Yes. Different people and genders, yet exactly the same thing happens. Once we start getting to know each other and the relationship starts getting a little serious, I start to get cold feet."

"What's the feeling when it happens, when you get 'cold feet' and shut people out?"

"At first, I feel anxious and scared. Then I feel very sad and sorrowful when I realize that once again it is over."

In my book, *Past Life Regression — A Manual for Hypnotherapists to Conduct Effective Past Life Regression Sessions*, I discussed how clients sometimes have a presenting issue and a self-diagnosed treatment plan[6]. In her case, Tomoko

---

[6] "Sometimes, though, a person may present a problem, and self-diagnose that the problem originated in a past life. Be cautious in this case. You can tell them that the problem may or may not have originated from a past life, but that together you can find out. Give them the option of starting by exploring a past life, which may possibly be the cause of their problem; or by focusing directly on the cause of their problem, which may also lead to a past life. Be clear with the person that their choice may influence what they get from the session. This way, client and therapist can make an informed decision together." | Excerpt from *Past Life Regression – A Manual for Hypnotherapists to Conduct Effective Past Life Regression Sessions,*

presented with difficulty in progressing in an intimate relationship and had a self-diagnosed treatment plan of a Past Life Regression. I had a feeling PLR *was* the right solution in her case.

Unbeknownst to Tomoko, she would prove to be an easy subject, despite saying, "I haven't had any déjà-vu experiences or any spontaneous childhood past life memories. I'm not sure about what I believe. I am only exploring." Tomoko had indicated as much on her intake form, having written "Spiritual? (Just exploring)" in the Religion field.

"Which is more important?" I asked, "Uncovering the cause for your feelings of fear and anxiety, sadness and sorrow? Or having a past life regression? Those may or may not lead us to the same place."

"Let's have a Past Life Regression. It's okay if we don't find out the reason for me shutting people out." I was a little surprised by Tomoko's decision. We had spent the last fifteen minutes focusing on and discussing her relationship issues. Like many of my clients, they are often more excited to explore a past life than dive into the more humdrum aspects of their original issues.

Having decided, Tomoko stretched out her legs on the recliner, readying herself to explore. Befitting someone new to a past life regression, I started softly and gently. I induced her subconscious mind to take us to a favourite place where she felt safe and at peace: "It can be anywhere inside or outside; any real place that you have been to, or any real place you wish to go; it can be an imagined place filled with all your favourite things."

Journey Beyond Publications, 2015, Kemila Zsange

Tomoko nodded her head slightly. "Is it inside, or is it outside?" I asked.

"It's outside." Her soft, quiet reply suggested Tomoko was already in a deep trance state.

"Yes, it is outside. Tell me, what's there?"

"It's a beach."

"Yes, it's a beach," I echoed.

"It's not *just* a beach. It's…" Tomoko paused, searching for illumination, "… It's… the secret beach I visited when I was a kid with my father and uncle!"

I had Tomoko fully immerse herself in the environment to activate all her senses. She proved to be an excellent hypnosis subject. Tomoko was very sensory-oriented, engaging sight, sound, and scent to describe her secret beach. It was a small pebble beach set amongst tree-lined crags. A trail descended through the rocks down to the secluded beach. Farther out to sea, the waves crashed against rocky outcrops, while on the shore, the receding tide crackled over round, sea-worn pebbles. The day was overcast, and the salty scent of ocean and forest permeated the air.

Showing all the signs of immersion, I had Tomoko open her eyes to examine them for signs of trance.

"That was very easy, wasn't it?"

"Yes. I could see very clearly where I was."

"Did that feel good being there?"

"Yes, very good. It was actually a beach that I went to in Japan when I was a kid. I had almost forgotten it."

When people say they "almost forgot" (consciously), I know that the memory is a gift from the unconscious mind. I also knew I was going to utilize it.

To build Tomoko's confidence, I said, "I want you to know that the past life regression experience is really no different from that secret beach experience. You will perceive it in exactly the same way. You will be able to see, hear, feel, and know in the moment. The same way you saw, heard, felt, and knew a moment ago. It will simply be just another time, maybe another place, living in another body, in another life. But how you experience it will be the same."

Tomoko nodded her head with understanding as I continued, "Since it feels so good on that secret beach, let's go back to it again, and let's take it a little further this time. Something is there that you will find that you didn't notice before, or maybe you overlooked it. But this time, you will be able to see it clearly."

On that cue, Tomoko slowly closed her eyes again. Slowing my patter, I said, "Yes, just walk around." Then I paused to let Tomoko sense and visualize the beach as she walked.

"And look." Pausing again. "Something is new. What's there?" I wondered whether anything would come up at all but spoke confidently, as though something *was* going to come up.

"There is a cave." Tomoko's voice came across as small and curious, yet confident.

A cave? I had no idea if it was a literal cave or a metaphorical one, something symbolic to Tomoko's subconscious. Regardless, her subconscious mind had been instructed to use the secret beach as the launching point for our time travel journey; I knew I would simply go with the flow.

"Yes. There is a cave there. Is the entrance big or small?"

"It's big enough to walk inside."

"Now, as you stand in front of the entrance to the cave, you look into it. Can you see inside?"

"No, it's dark."

"Yes. It is dark. How do you feel about the cave?"

"I feel scared, but I do want to go and look inside."

Just like when she first contacted me, I thought. *Curious, eager, and anxious, all at the same time. Or like when she starts a new relationship, curious, keen to explore it at the beginning, despite knowing of her inevitable feelings of disquiet and sorrow if it were to progress beyond the casual stage.*

I had Tomoko manifest a flashlight in her hand and indicated for her to enter the cave with it. And in the other hand, she manifested a walking staff to help stabilize her on the uneven terrain. Or to be used for protection, if so needed.

With her well-equipped, it was now time to let Tomoko travel into another life. Almost imperceptibly, the cave morphed into and became a portal, a doorway into her past. Slowly, I guided Tomoko into the cave, weaving the inside of the cave into her innermost relationship vulnerabilities.

"As you know, when a relationship has developed to a certain degree, you start to feel hesitant, anxious and scared. And finally, sad and sorrowful. It is a similar feeling as you allow yourself to enter this cave. Connect with those emotions and continue moving ever deeper into the cave. In a moment, when I count from 5 to 1, but only when I reach the number 1, your flashlight will flicker, and the cave will take you into another scene, a new scene. Another time, maybe another life that has everything to do with these emotions. Yes. You have a question, and this cave holds an answer. It will take you to where you need to go today to find the answer."

Counting down to one, Tomoko easily flowed into a scene. She could not help but laugh a little because she landed back on another beach!

It felt long ago, like Roman times, and Tomoko was a male named Andrea. He was walking, hand in hand, with his lover, Ore, feeling the full depth and breadth of their love for one another. Ore was an artist in his late twenties; Andrea, who was second-in-command in the army, was in his early thirties. The two had met in their teens and had secretly met up on that secluded beach ever since. A place they privately referred to as their "secret beach." *Perhaps, Tomoko called the beach that her father and uncle had taken her to as a child the "secret beach" because there was this memory of love hidden mysteriously deep within her,* I postulated.

That day on their beach, Ore was in a playful mode, but Andrea was feeling torn apart by a secret he had been harbouring from his lover. His captain was arranging for Andrea to marry the captain's sister. Sad and anxious, Andrea had decided today would be the day he finally shared his news with Ore. That confession was presumably why Tomoko's subconscious had taken us to this opening scene on the beach.

Ore begged and pleaded with his lover not to marry. Desperate, Ore suggested they escape to a small, far away, and little-known island where his family lived, where they would be safe and could start a new life together. Andrea saw things differently.

"Ore doesn't understand the depth of my responsibility. I cannot betray my country," he reasoned. More importantly, Andrea was terrified. "If I don't marry the captain's sister, someone will find out about Ore and me. And my captain may kill us both."

Andrea saw only one feasible course of action: to end their relationship. The time had come when they could no longer see each other anymore.

"I *hate* this decision! I *love* him so much!" Andrea sobbed while confessing his love for Ore. Nonetheless, the childhood sweethearts sorrowfully parted ways. True to his word, Andrea married his captain's sister; and the couple had two children together.

Twenty years passed. The children grew up and left home to make their own way in the world. Duty-bound, Andrea was miserable. He thought of and missed Ore with every passing day.

"Scan into your future from this moment on," I instructed. "Do you ever get to see Ore again?"

Andrea paused briefly, then answered, "It's hard to tell. I think I saw him once, in a crowd. It was for a few seconds. Then I lost him. Or maybe it wasn't even him, and I only hoped it was..." His voice faded.

Fifty years after their fateful meeting, Andrea walked along their secret beach, a cane marking his slow course across the pebbly sand. Now in his eighties, his unhappiness had turned into a dysthymic melancholy. And in that moment on their beach, Andrea wished he had never left Ore. *Could this be the reason why Tomoko was so afraid to fall in love?* I wondered. *As they say, love hurts.* I knew I had been granted an opportunity to help Tomoko put her pain and anguish behind her by changing that past life. When we can visualize an alternative in a past life regression and let what I call "parallel life[7]" play out, we regain our power of choice. And this time, Andrea was going to choose *love.*

"Stay right here on this beach, Andrea. Looking back many decades, knowing what you know now, if you could do

---

[7] More information on Parallel Life, Probable Parallel Reality, and Alternative Life Path can be read in the Chapter Just Do It.

it again, on this same beach all that time ago, would you choose differently?"

"Yes."

"Because 50 years ago, you didn't know better. You thought 'duty' was something more important, and you feared the alternative. But now you know better. How would you choose differently?"

"I would... I don't know how... I would quit my job and go off with him."

"To the little island where Ore had family?"

"Yes."

"That would be a risk you would take then, wouldn't it?"

"Yes."

"Tell me then, Andrea, why is it worth taking such a risk?"

"Ore was my soulmate."

"What about your duty to the army, to your captain?"

"If I quit the army, I would not carry the weight of that responsibility." Now, Andrea's voice came through with strength and clarity, "The duty only comes with the job. The way the army works, someone else would be promoted to my position, and that person might be a better choice than me for that role anyway."

I decided to let the soul guide us and have it just play out. A different memory needed to be activated from her life as Andrea to encourage a different behaviour pattern for Tomoko's subconscious. The subconscious deals in the realm of emotions, actions, and beliefs. So, I needed to shift the emotions associated with relationships, freeing Tomoko to choose different actions.

I asked the older Andrea if he could find a place on that beach to rest. Andrea scanned the beach and spotted a large outcrop under a tree where he might rest and lean his cane.

"Go there now and sit down. Rest your body and invite a feeling of calmness and relaxation to wash over you. Just as the ocean washes over the rocks on the shore, it is the same place, but at a different time. And sitting there under the tree, you start to wonder if time might rewind itself." I paused, letting my words sink in, letting time unwind. "In your vision now… On that same beach…" I trailed off. "If you could do it again, and you somehow step into a bubble of that new reality." I waited for a moment, allowing the possibility of an alternative reality to surface in Andrea's consciousness. Then I continued, "And stepping into that bubble reality, on that same beach, you are in your early 30's again, and Ore is in his late twenties. You are there talking about your future. You share with him that the captain is arranging for you to marry his sister. You do feel a strong sense of duty and responsibility to the country, but you hate having to make this choice, although you feel you *do* need to make it.

"Ore is begging you to run away with him to that island where his family lives. He is telling you that it is not that he does not understand your responsibilities. But you know you can only be responsible *after* you have made the decision to remain in that position."

I had set up the probable parallel reality for Andrea. All that was left was to present him with the opportunity to accept it: "As you allow yourself to ponder these choices, these possible futures, at the same time and in the back of your mind, you know, if you choose duty over love how your life will turn out. You have identified Ore as your soulmate. You want to be with him. There is so much love you have experienced with him." And in that parallel reality regression, Andrea not only pondered the possibility, but he also took inspired action.

Andrea notified his captain that he would be resigning from his position as second-in-command and that he would not be marrying his sister. Upon hearing this, his captain was furious, scaring Andrea.

Counselling Andrea, I offered, "Inside you, there is something far stronger than that anger or even fear. There is the great love that you feel. You can be honest; you just tell the truth. The truth is you do not love his sister. It would not be good for his sister to marry you."

"I told him I have a different plan for my life. I will leave all my weapons behind and simply walk away. He's not being rational, and I don't need to convince him."

Andrea's abrupt decisions shocked everyone. Marrying the captain's sister was a prized social status to achieve and considered a type of promotion. All the soldiers stared in disbelief as they watched him walk away. But Andrea no longer cared about such things. The farther away Andrea got from his old life and obligations, the lighter he felt with each new step forward. The feeling surprised him. He had believed being a soldier was *everything*, and now that he was not, he felt *free*.

Not to do things halfway, Andrea told his family of his secret and immediate plans. The surprises were not yet over for Andrea. His two siblings happily shared with him what they already knew. They had wagered that their brother was in love with a man, and now, one of them had won.

Andrea thought he had a huge secret, yet it seemed those who loved him had known. In a way, it was they who held a secret. He began to wonder why he had not told them sooner. Everyone in his family was relieved to hear the news that Andrea had finally chosen to follow his heart. Everyone, save his father. Andrea's father was upset that his son had resigned from a respected post.

Sometimes we think we know how our families will react, but their compassion and understanding take us by surprise. Might Andrea have confided in his family sooner; their loving support could have made facing his captain easier.

Telling our truth is always an opportunity. It can hold space for others to choose their responses, what they want to do, and most importantly, who they want to be. In Andrea's case, his family chose to be loving and kind. Even Andrea's father eventually understood his reasons for quitting and shrugged off his dismay to share in the joy with the rest of his family.

Finally free to emerge from their shell, Ore and Andrea moved to the island, just as a safety precaution against the captain's presumed wrath. Upon their arrival, Ore's father openly accepted Andrea. In contrast, Ore's mother was a little cold and harsh towards her son's lover at the beginning. But Andrea felt happy and free, living with Ore, helping out on Ore's family farm.

Many contented years passed on their tiny island home before Andrea began to feel homesick. He wanted his family to meet his soulmate. So, the couple set out on the long, arduous journey back to Andrea's family on the mainland; they travelled for days by foot and by boat. At long last, they arrived and found only a ghost town where the city had once been. In the face of a hostile invasion, the city's residents had fled their homes and places of work in the desperate hope of saving their lives. Many buildings stood damaged or destroyed by the marauding troops. Andrea's family home, though, could still be seen amidst the rubble.

Slowly, some of the city's inhabitants had begun to return. Through one of the returnees, Andrea learned his family had escaped the carnage and had settled in a distant town. His spirits rose with the news of his family's escape. Desiring to see his family and confirm that they were indeed safe, he decided to go and search for them. There were no guarantees of how long the journey would take, what he might discover along the way, or even if it would be safe. Ore chose to go with his lover, and they set out on yet another journey. The couple travelled for more than a month before locating Andrea's family living in a small mountain village. His mother and siblings were safe and unharmed, but his father had perished amidst the conflict. Andrea's family was shocked to see Andrea again. Their shock soon gave way to tears of joy and relief, with tears giving way to heartfelt embraces.

Ore became a loved and accepted member of Andrea's family, and soon after the family's joyful reunion, the couple settled in and began discussing their incredible journey. They found they had both enjoyed the experience of travelling. It had been fun, and the allure of further adventure called to them both. They resolved to grow their love more deeply and live their lives more fully through continued exploration of their world. Thus, theirs became a life wholly and richly lived— leaving Andrea feeling happy and complete.

I had Andrea's awareness return to the secret beach whence he entered his parallel reality bubble and joined with the energy already present there. Carrying with him a life abounding with contentment, discovery, and adventure; of moving forward, following his heart, and exploring the depth and width of a life open to new experiences. An inner light formed inside the soul as the energies joined. In the light, there was only divine clarity.

Tomoko would share that the energy of Ore was not present in her life—at least not yet. Maybe the next love who shows up could be that soulmate. Or perhaps, not. Upon revisiting her secret beach, Tomoko felt only openness and relief.

Lay down your weapons and stride away.
The choice to be vulnerable is a show of your strength.
Be you, full you. All else will take care of itself.
As you say, love heals.

Tomoko emerged from her trance with the biggest smile, "Oh my God. That was incredible!"

Yesterday and Tomorrow's Child

A Struggle Between Eagerness and Anxiety

In my profession, there is a popular misconception that accountants and lawyers are among the most challenging people to hypnotize because they possess overly analytical minds. In many cases, that may be true. However, I have been fortunate. I have worked with many clients from both professions and have generally found them as hypnotizable as anyone else.

Sandy was an accountant who described herself as a classic Type A personality, someone who tirelessly strives for perfection. Her presenting issue was anxiety, especially concerning infertility. Sandy was so nervous coming in for her appointment that she could not keep her eyes closed long enough to begin the hypnotic induction. I assured her that "hypnosis is not a matter of eyelids," that she could keep her eyes open if it made her feel more comfortable. And so, we began our first session with Sandy's anxious eyes wide open.

With her eyes gazing at a spot on the ceiling and while reclining comfortably in the chair, I guided Sandy to move her focus inward. She started to describe an intense, physical sensation in the pit of her stomach: anxiety.

"Rather than fighting that sensation or running away from that sensation, as you normally might, imagine going *inside* that sensation in your stomach... You will not be alone; my voice will be here with you every step of the way. Now dive down into that sensation, deep within your belly." At that juncture in our session, I intentionally kept using the words "that sensation" rather than "anxiety."

Sandy complied trepidatiously, confessing after entering that sensation that she eventually "landed" in a light-filled space. I have often observed one can enter a dark, tense emotion, like anxiety and then find themselves in a bright and expansive space. Following my instruction, Sandy played with the light "with nothing other than curiosity."

Some time passed with Sandy curiously playing in that light space, and eventually, she expressed her need to use the washroom. I counted her up from 1 to 3 and instructed her to have enough awareness to do what her body needed to do. Sandy appeared calmer when she returned and told me that the sensation of anxiety in her stomach had gone. And that she would like to come back for some follow-up sessions. Again, I was amazed by the subconscious mind's self-healing abilities.

There was just enough time in our session to quickly put Sandy back into a trance and give her a post-hypnotic suggestion to re-enter the hypnotic state with greater ease when she returned to work with me.

We set up another four appointments over the coming weeks and discussed meditation as a relaxation tool. Sandy agreed that meditation might indeed help her relax more, but she was so busy with her work that she could not see how she would find the time. To practice getting out of her head, I suggested that she contemplate the question: *Who Am I?* as a part of her nightly sleep routine. "Your mind will quickly jump in and give you all the easy answers, like your name, your profession, and your relationship. But tell your mind, *'I know that'* and continue to ask yourself, *'Who am I really?'* Like a mantra, just keep coming back to that question, again and again.

"Before you know it, you will be meditating yourself into a wonderful sleep. And it won't even take any time out of your busy schedule."

A week later, Sandy came back for her second appointment, reporting that the *Who Am I?* sleep assignment had been most beneficial in calming her nerves. The bedtime practice had helped her so well that she was far more relaxed for our work. This time around, Sandy closed her eyes with a willingness and ease.

A childhood memory surfaced. It was unpleasant and sexual, something Sandy had consciously, only "sort of" remembered but was too ashamed and kept the details at bay. Using the safety net of hypnosis, we looked at the memory and neutralized its charge in her adult self by accepting, embracing, and reassuring her child self.

"Just like a good parent would do," I offered Sandy by way of suggestion; Sandy was eager to be a mother. I continued, "Because now you have the capacity and ability to be the parent for your inner child first."

Sandy's third session found us utilizing Parts Therapy. We spoke to both the part of Sandy that wanted a child and the part that was hesitant and doubtful. The skeptical part was allowed to express its doubts about having the capacity or personal strength to care for a human baby. A responsibility Sandy described as "huge." Her inner skeptic doubted whether her relationship with her husband would survive having a child; whether it was strong enough to sustain the family and a growing child. As the negotiation of parts continued, the part that desperately wanted a child agreed to go more slowly, not to rush into having a child, so long as the skeptical part was willing to move towards having a baby. While acknowledging and giving expression to the conflicting parts of Sandy, we succeeded in having both aspects agree on taking "baby steps" moving forward.

I received a surprising message from Sandy before our fourth session. She confided that she had finally come to terms with whether she got pregnant and asked if we could do a past life regression to address her general anxiety. To date, we had not discussed past lives. So, I had been unaware that she might be open to this possibility. But I gladly agreed, telling Sandy that it usually would be a good idea to try and find the source of anxiety through regression. However, she indicated that her anxiety was "general," and I was skeptical about whether regression would be the best way to target it. Or whether we would indeed land in a past life through that avenue. If she was still keen to do a regression, my alternative plan was to have her experience what it felt like to be a mother in a past life. Sandy eagerly agreed to my alternative approach.

By Sandy's fourth session, I was confident she had developed into a rather good hypnotic subject. So, I simply instructed Sandy to gently close her eyes, allowing her subconscious mind to take us where we needed to go. Then I began my monotone narrative: "While we have been having this conversation, your unconscious mind has been on board, knowing exactly where to take us for our exploration…"

Sandy was Margaret, a proud woman in her sixties with salt and pepper hair. She was sitting on a bench in a charming little park near her home. I guided Margaret back to her house to see who else might live there: she sat at a round, ornate wooden table having dinner with her husband, who usually remained at home and did most of the cooking. "He's tall and looking very grave, wearing his burgundy vest. Oh, and he has a moustache! That's so funny! His name is Tony," Margaret happily described her partner, replete with Sandy's running commentary.

"Look into Tony's eyes. Do you have an instant recognition of this person from Sandy's life?"

"Ha! Yes. He is my husband, even though my husband does not have a moustache." Sandy giggled.

"Are there any other family members at the dinner table?"

"No. It's just him and I. He is sitting across from me. We have a son, although he no longer lives with us. But—" Margaret hesitated, "I don't know why I keep seeing this girl."

"You keep seeing this girl. Describe her."

"She isn't human. Maybe a ghost? She is awfully white. All over. And she is sitting here at the table with us."

I was surprised. "You don't seem to be disturbed by her." People often have adverse reactions toward the paranormal. "How old does the girl appear to be?"

"About 12 years old. She's just sitting there, not eating."

Well, I thought, *one does need a body to eat.* "As you look at her, does she look at you, too?"

"Yes. She is looking at me now."

"Does Tony notice her too?"

"No. He is eating his dinner, unaware. I don't think he sees her. Or maybe he just pretends not to see her."

"Ask the girl why she is sitting there."

"She says I'm her mom."

Margaret, it seemed, had a daughter who died at twelve. I realized this could be the cause of Sandy's pregnancy anxiety.

Given the age of Margaret and Tony, and the mention of an adult son, their daughter must have died a long time ago.

I took Margaret farther back in time to when her daughter died: It was nighttime, and Tony was driving the family car with their daughter sitting in the front passenger seat next to him. Just father and daughter, alone in the car, together. This was the era long before seat belts, ample street lighting, and airbags. The road was dark, and Tony lost control of the car.

Margaret's husband survived the crash, but her daughter perished. Driven by overwhelming guilt, Tony sank into a deep depression for many years. Four years after the tragic accident, Margaret gave birth to their second child, a son. Generally a joyous occasion for a father, Tony could not bring himself to make a hospital appearance to welcome his son.

Whether it was the pain of losing his firstborn that stopped Tony from opening up again or a way to protect his boy from himself, Tony's son grew up with an emotionally distant and unavailable father.

"Since your daughter died, her ghost has remained with you?"

"Yes. She was there too when her baby brother was born," Margaret replied. Margaret was comfortable having the familiar ghost of her daughter around all the time.

"Do you know, it may not be the best place for her? She has lost her body. There can be a better place for her to be. Ask her if she would like to leave?"

Margaret paused before replying, "She says 'No.' This is her home. She doesn't know where else to go."

"What about you? Would you like her to go?"

"I'm okay either way. I feel she doesn't even know that she's dead. She's saying she is going to be with me no matter

what. I suppose she will just go with me once I die." I
respected Margaret's choice and decided not to push her any
further on the matter.

We moved forward in time to Margaret's last moment on
Earth: She found herself in her seventies, lying alone in a
hospital bed. Reminiscent of the day their son was born,
Tony remained at home. After taking her last breath and
leaving her body behind, the spirit visited her son. It was
surprised to find him weeping, almost as though her son
intuitively knew his mother had just passed away. The spirit
moved onward and forward into the light. I made sure it took
the spirit of the little girl with her.

Upon emerging from hypnosis, I shared my observations
with Sandy, "The difficulty of getting pregnant may not be
because of you, Sandy. But with your husband."

"That's unbelievable!" Sandy exclaimed, with eyes now
wide open. "The doctors just recently found—I guess it's
okay to get a little personal here—that physically, it's not me
but my husband. His sperm count is low. He's just started a
new procedure."

I contemplated aloud, "It would be interesting… If your
husband could come to see me for a past life regression. We
could take the opportunity to discover what comes out of his
side of the story."

"Okay. I will speak with him. Although, I doubt if he
would be open to this kind of work. Oh my God!" Sandy
placed a hand to her mouth, "I remember something. Once,
out of the blue, my husband asked, 'What if we have a child
and then she dies at 12 years old?' I always felt it was strange
a thing for him to say." I felt it was anything but strange
when hearing Sandy connecting the dots to those seemingly

random, strange, yet entirely relatable memories. My work often crosses linear timelines. Hundreds of my clients have trained me to observe and recognize patterns as they emerge. An inner knowingness arises inside me—call it intuition— that is so powerful that there is no room for doubt when it occurs. In that moment, I knew that Sandy's past-life daughter intended to come through to be her daughter in this lifetime. Sandy was ready, her daughter had been waiting a long time, but her husband was hesitant. Caught between her unconceived daughter's eagerness and her husband's nervous hesitancy, Sandy had a lot of excitable energy in her stomach. In her day-to-day living, that energy presented as general anxiety.

By trade, I am a registered hypnotherapist, not a psychic, but I am a highly intuitive person. And at times, I cannot help knowing what I *know*, inherently. I decided not to say much about it to Sandy and simply told her that if she agreed, we could tap into a probable future in this life in our last session together. Something we call a Future Life Progression.

Sandy showed up to our last session bearing great news: her husband's treatment was going very well. To help lower his anxiety about possibly having a daughter, she comforted him by telling him she felt it would most likely be a boy. Satisfied with her approach, Sandy reclined comfortably in the chair, drifted into a very relaxed state, and entered deep hypnosis.

Sandy took us into a future scene in a small park close to her home. A mother and father were blissfully enjoying a picnic with their young child. The happy family lounged in the warmth of a perfectly sunny summer's day. A smiling toddler sat on the brightly patterned picnic blanket between the proud parents. It was future Sandy, her husband, and their daughter. In that future life, Sandy was finally a mother again.

Part 2 – Discovering Inner Gifts

Finding a soul's unique expression through past life regression

DISCOVER verb (used with object)

- to see, get knowledge of, learn of, find, or find out; gain sight or knowledge of (something or someone previously unseen or unknown)
- to divulge (a secret)

Pain Body, Wolf, Ghosts, and Laughter

Beautifully Unexpected Outcomes

Pauline researched physical pain and the role the subconscious mind plays in pain, focusing primarily on "pain caused by accidents." During her Google research, Pauline came across a 2015 blog post of mine called, *A Dialogue with "Pain Body" in Hypnotherapy* and reached out to me.

I was a little surprised that someone would initiate a session with me based on that article about pain-body. My article did not discuss the aspects of physical pain at all. Nonetheless, Pauline was very eager. So much so that when she booked her session online, she accidentally sent the payment twice.

"I know you spoke about psychological pain in your article," Pauline began our video session. "And the concept of 'pain body' you mentioned comes from Eckhart Tolle, of whom I have read a lot. So, I understand the concept. But I still want to work with you as I am experiencing a lot of physical pain. Let me explain."

Pauline had always been a highly active person. She loved sports and exercising. Holding a Ph.D. and working as an independent consultant, Pauline travelled all over the world, teaching short courses to academics.

In past years, the middle-aged woman had suffered several accidents. Once an accident had occurred, another would follow. It had become an agonizing cycle of pain and recovery. First, she had a skiing accident. While still healing from that, Pauline went sledding and injured her left knee. An accidental tearing of a tendon in her right shoulder followed soon after. It was an unrelenting pain that disturbed Pauline's sleep and kept her up at night. And then, more recently, she had fallen and badly bruised both her legs.

From a young age, Pauline was aware of some sort of mental-emotional connection to her frequent accidents: if she had a "bad thought," Pauline would fall or hurt herself. Now in her late fifties, Pauline was frustrated and tired of regularly being in pain. Her husband worried about her constantly, never knowing what the extent or the timing of his wife's next injury might be.

Having heard why Pauline was seeking my help, I guided her into a hypnotic trance while Pauline's breathing shifted into a slow, deep rhythm. We went through a progressive relaxation, paying particular attention to her left knee, right shoulder, and legs; I was setting up a dialogue with the part of Pauline that knew why her accidents had occurred. When the time was right, I invited the part to come forth and speak with me. Surprisingly, the part identified itself as "Child."

"Child, how old are you?"

"Two." Pauline showed up scared and sobbing on the screen of my iPad.

"Little Two, tell me what is going on?"

"I… I am scared of the Wolf," Child explained in between tears.

"The wolf?" I decided to play along, "What does the wolf do that scares you, Child?"

"It's dark. The Wolf likes to scare me. I don't know what to do. I can only hide. I want to become smaller and smaller, so hopefully, he doesn't see me."

"Can you do that, Child? Become smaller and smaller?"

"No. He always sees me and terrorizes me! It's a terrorizing creature!"

"What does the terrorizing creature want from you, Child?"

"I don't know…. Oh! He wants my soul!"

"That is right. The wolf wants your soul because you have a soul, and perhaps he does not." Pauline, shaking and crying, crawled herself up into a fetal position. I continued to guide her the way I would speak with a little child, "I want you to breathe deeply now. And I want you to know, Child, that anyone with a soul is 100 times stronger than those who don't. That's why the wolf wants to terrorize you. He appears as having power over you, but your soul is where the power is.

"Now, Child, is this the first time that the wolf has terrorized you? Or have you had this experience before?"

"It's not the first time. He has shown up many, many times before."

"Yes. Many times, the wolf has threatened you. He said he was going to take your soul. Or even maybe he was going to kill you?"

Pauline nodded her head in agreement.

"But you are still here. Alive, with your soul. I know you are only two years old, but you are a smart one, aren't you? Can you see that the wolf cannot actually do what he says he is going to do? That he can only say it?"

Pauline nodded her head again and soon stopped sobbing. Her tone changed, the adult-self assuming its primary position, "Eighty percent of me understands what you are saying. Still, there is a twenty percent that is very scared."

I love it when a client gives me both a clue and the direction in a session: "All right. I am speaking to the twenty percent right now. I know you are very scared. I also know you are a *very* important part of Pauline. What I want to tell you is that it is okay to be scared." Suddenly, adult Pauline's facial expression changed, and she crawled herself back up into a ball, tears streaming down her face. She looked like a helpless two-year-old again. I continued to soothe the child Pauline, "That's right. It's okay to be scared. And you can let it all out now. Very soon, you will feel much better and lighter after you have cried it all out. And then you can tell me, what *exactly* scares you?"

"*Them.* The ghosts. They scare me."

"Ghosts!" We were just one week before Halloween. Although Pauline lived in Europe, and Halloween is essentially a North American tradition, I reasoned the well-travelled woman would understand— "I bet you don't like Halloween."

"No! I'm always terrified to sleep by myself. Sometimes I hear the ghosts. I can feel a cold, chilly sense when they are around." Eyes still closed, her body straightening and tone changing as she shifted back into her adult self, Pauline said, "Now I remember... I remember my family house when I was a kid. I was always terrified by the basement. Especially when I went down there by myself."

"What was it about the basement that terrified you?"

"I could feel something was not right there. And I remember another time we hired a psychic who confirmed that our house was haunted. But before that, my family didn't believe me. I was just so scared."

"Was the psychic scared of the ghosts?"

"No, she was not."

"But you are, aren't you?"

"I'm not a psychic. I don't have psychic powers."

"Do you know those ghosts?"

"No! It's scary."

"Since you don't know them, this may not be a fear of ghosts but a fear of the unknown."

I was about to say that as we were all souls, in a way we were all 'ghosts' living in a human body, but Pauline was nodding her head in complete agreement, so I ventured on, "This is a fear of the unknown… Remember that wolf who wanted to feel empowered by having your soul? You *are* a soulful being. Your soul is your light. I want you to find your soul now and, therefore, find your light."

Pauline's face softened, and she smiled, "Yeah, I'm feeling much better now."

"That's right. Now I want you to wear your soul as your jacket. Feel that light all around you as you wear this jacket of light. Because of your soul, everywhere you go now, it will be full of light. You do understand, don't you?"

"Yes. I do."

"Now, wearing your 'soul jacket' of light and with the sound of my voice, let's go down to the basement of your family home. You don't have to rush. Let's go down slowly, as slowly as you comfortably can. Like a child tiptoeing into a swimming pool, make sure with every step you take that you are safe."

"Yes, I'm there now." *Well, that was even faster than I was about to guide.*

"Now that you are there, and the place is not dark anymore because of your light, what do you see?"

"I see a little girl."

"A little girl. How old is she?"

"She's about five."

"What is she doing?"

"She's just standing there, in the washing machine area."

"Now you are seeing her. Does she see you?"

"She saw me. But the moment she saw me, she started to drift away…"

"Interesting. You never thought about that, did you? It's as if she's afraid of you. The *ghost* is afraid of *you*!"

"No. I never thought about that!"

"That's how powerful you are. Maybe you are psychic, after all."

"No. I am not," Pauline insisted.

"So, you are sensitive enough to see ghosts but not psychic enough to know them. Therefore, you often get caught up in fear."

"Exactly, that's it."

"You know, my eyes can see," I was unsure where I was going with this, but I ran with it, "and when I close my eyes, I don't see. But just because I don't see with my eyelids closed doesn't mean I need to call myself blind."

Pauline burst out into loud laughter. She laughed so hard that her eyes popped open, and she brought herself out of her trance, becoming fully awake and aware. Pauline continued to laugh like that for a good 10-minutes, wiping her face with tissues. Her laughter was contagious, and soon, I was laughing along with Pauline. Laughter truly is the best medicine. I knew Pauline was centering herself, the eighty percent and twenty percent parts integrating and coming together organically.

Bowing her head deep, Pauline finally stopped laughing, "I think that's it for today's session. I know the time is not up yet, but I have got what I need and so much more!" Pauline started to laugh again, and we both signed off. Just when you think you know who you are, you find out more. Who knows? Pauline might not only be psychic but a comedienne, as well.

One day later, I received an email from Pauline:

"Dear Kemila,

Thank you soooooooooooooooooooo much for yesterday!

It is interesting there were some snags (from my subconscious/something else) with paying for my session with you. And still, we succeeded with a beautiful and totally unexpected outcome.

Then 30 minutes later, beautiful synchronicity happened. I'm part of an online healing group that meets every Tuesday. I had not mentioned the outcome from our session, but the topic suggested for that group was Becoming Increasingly Clairvoyant!!!! (And for the first time in my life, I wasn't terrified by the thought of this!)

Thank you vastly!!!!! It was so lovely to work with you. You were the perfect person to help me with what I needed!!!!!!!!

With lots of love, Pauline"

Coaching A Ghost

Acknowledging Past Companions

Who would think you could coach a ghost? Certainly not Carolina, who was completing her life coaching practicum. Carolina had contacted me to work through her anger issues. During our initial Skype call, I mentioned that prolonged anger is often an indicator of something much deeper.

"That's why I'm calling you," the 35-year-old explained. "I've been thinking about hypnotherapy for a while now. I've seen a psychologist before to treat issues of insecurity and low self-confidence. And I know my anger is connected to me having high expectations of myself and others. But I just don't know how to let it go. I also want to look deeper into my anger's emotional and spiritual causes." *Spiritual causes?* My ears are like radar. They know certain words to detect, and "spiritual" is one of those words. What do people mean by "spiritual"? My curiosity was piqued, and I had to know more.

Spirituality is the foundation of a person's life journey, and knowing their spirituality helps me choose the language to use when working with them. When a client identifies as "non-spiritual," that in and of itself is part of a foundational belief system that can inform my choice of words. I can only follow paths that are in my client's awareness. Without data points or more context, I cannot assume where specific emotions originate from, nor can I assume how to resolve them.

Born and raised in Ecuador, Carolina was a lovely fusion of White, Indigenous, Black, "and about eight percent Chinese." Though not religious, she believed in life beyond death, expressing interest in past life regression. "Souls coming back," like reincarnation, made more sense to Carolina than not.

Bringing our Skype call to a close, we agreed to schedule a series of five sessions. I then asked Carolina if she had any final questions for me.

"Will I have to share everything in a session?" Carolina asked. *What an interesting question,* I thought. *Why would someone want to withhold something potentially relevant for healing from their own therapist?*

"No, you won't have to," I replied. "What are you concerned about?"

"Well," Carolina began, "I keep wondering if things will come up in hypnosis that I might be afraid to tell you."

In all my years of practice, with many clients over numerous sessions, I have heard a great deal of strange, weird, wonderful, other-worldly, cruel, and embarrassing things. But I focused on the most likely reason for Carolina's concern, so I offered, "You mean embarrassing things?"

"I don't know. Maybe in hypnosis, I'll lose control. Maybe I'll say things that I may not consciously want to say."

I knew Carolina was alluding to something specific, but I did not yet understand what or why. So, I simply told her that content-free hypnosis was entirely possible. I reassured her that her subconscious mind was also the protective mind; it would not say anything to me that she was not willing to share.

Carolina's first session brought me the happy discovery that she was one of those clients who are a joy to work with: she was self-aware, possessing valuable personal insights. I could easily see why Carolina had chosen a career path as a life coach. Typically, a client's first session focuses on the diagnostic process and developing a treatment plan. Carolina's heightened self-awareness greatly aided this process. During our initial session, Carolina even displayed an ideomotor response—an unconscious finger twitching movement in response to a hypnotist's yes/no questions—her subconscious mind revealing that there were indeed past lives to review.

It wasn't until our next session, just as we started the hypnosis process, that she felt feelings of fear immediately arise: "What is the fear, Carolina? Is it fear of being hypnotized?" I queried.

"It's like embarrassment, but that's not the right word. It's difficult for me to voice it. It's this darkness that I feel around me sometimes. And sometimes I feel..." Carolina paused, shifting her seat and looking uncomfortable. "Sometimes, I feel that the darkness is *inside* me." She stopped again before exclaiming fearfully, "What if the darkness really comes *from* me?!"

"So, are you afraid that hypnotherapy may confirm that feeling for you? Is that your fear?"

"Maybe."

I had my own thoughts about "darkness," but at that point, Carolina simply needed to be reassured of the safety and security of the process. Rather than launching into a discussion about "the darkness," I assured Carolina that she was always in control, inside and outside of hypnosis, and that we would not go anywhere her conscious or subconscious minds did not wish us to go.

Fear is a curious thing; the fear of being a dark force is even more so. Didn't *feeling* fear already signal to Carolina that she was not innately dark? Simply expressing concern about its possibility, instead of blindly accepting it, denoted the darkness could not be Carolina's true self. If it were, there would be only total and complete acceptance of the fact, not fear or anger or shame. Feeling bad about "being" bad indicates that badness is not an ingrained part of our identity. It reminded me of the opening lines of the *Serenity Prayer*[8] and how it spoke of the wisdom in being aware of our scope of influence and control. Knowing we can only control ourselves and encouraging a willingness to release resistant feelings, like shame or embarrassment, anger or frustration, fear or being bad, that arise when we will not accept that which is not within our power to change.

We, humans, contain such a vast capacity for change. Those things we can change and the emotions connected to them can provide us with the inspiration and courage to effect growth and positive change.

Carolina came back every week reporting that the therapy was working, and her anger was lessening with each session. I kept her concerns about her darkness in mind, but I did not bring it up to unpack before she was truly ready. There is a right timing for everything. Pushing too early and wanting to "heal" a person before their readiness is in place can have a remarkably negative impact.

The opportunity to further explore Carolina's fear finally presented itself a few sessions later. We had travelled to a past life through hypnosis and then arrived at an inter-life. There Carolina had met her spirit guide, Gladys. Fancying myself a sort of right-timing ninja, I deftly seized my opportunity and

---

[8] Reinhold Niebuhr's, Serenity Prayer, 1926: "God, grant me the serenity to accept the things I cannot change, Courage to change the things I can, and the wisdom to know the difference."

posed my question to Spirt Guide Gladys: "What is the darkness that seems to come *from* Carolina?" There was a slight pause as Carolina channelled, then Gladys' answer came clear and true: "There is no such a thing as darkness," the guide stated. *Perfect!* I thought. *Now it is time for Carolina to know this herself and to really hear it.* She emerged from hypnosis, remembering everything that had taken place in that past and inter-life, coming away from the experience with a sense of having gained great clarity.

Carolina's last session saw her introducing the concept of managing expectations: her expectations towards others and how specific individuals treated her as though she were not an adult. Carolina detested not being taken seriously by others. Ironically, she did not sound confident when I encouraged her to challenge her own beliefs around these concerns.

Shortly before our final appointment, Carolina conducted a coaching session with one of her clients. She had been helpful and walked away from that session with the feeling of becoming a good coach. Piggybacking off that experience and those feelings, I suggested that Carolina could coach herself by setting up two chairs at home and switching back and forth between the two chairs to play the dual roles of client and coach. Carolina laughed at my suggestion, "I don't know how serious I would take myself if I tried to coach myself in that way." *Wait a minute! Wasn't that one of Carolina's problems— not being taken seriously by others?*

"Perhaps, others don't take you seriously because *you* don't take *yourself* seriously. If you cannot coach yourself, then it must not be easy. Now at least you can understand others for not taking you seriously," I challenged the coach. And choosing to take another tack, I suggested that she might find it more helpful if I taught her some self-hypnosis. Then she might role-play in hypnosis without feeling so self-conscious. Carolina willingly agreed to the compromise.

We practiced a simple self-hypnosis technique several times until Carolina could easily go into hypnosis independently.

"What if I can't snap myself out of hypnosis?" she asked while we were practicing.

"You can always count yourself from 0 to 5 out of hypnosis," I replied.

"Another question: What if, when I practice the self-hypnosis on my own, I go to a bad place?"

And there it was. I felt that we had established enough rapport, that Carolina had gained enough trust in the process and exercised and strengthened enough spiritual muscles to now face her fear head-on. In our fifth and final session together, I could sense Carolina was ready for *something*.

I told Carolina we would address her concern in a moment after a little more self-hypnosis practice. Carolina obliged and practiced her self-hypnosis technique, putting herself into a deep hypnotic state. "In a moment, I will ask you to open your eyes," I started the induction. "When your eyes are open, you will remain in this state. But you will stand up, move across the space and take the chair I am sitting on, and I will stand up and take the seat you are sitting in. Once we have exchanged seats, the moment you sit down, you will instantly become Life Coach Carolina. You will speak with the person in front of you, a person who has a problem of not being taken seriously, not growing up, and not meeting her and others' expectations. You, as Life Coach Carolina, will start to speak immediately, and you will know exactly what to say to help the person in front of you." The moment Carolina sat down on my chair, and I sat on the couch mimicking her posture, she leaned forward, looked at me in my eyes, and asked, "When was the last time you spoke with your father?"

My mind paused. I, the client, had no clue, but I took a guess and said, "A while ago."

Carolina smiled, "I think it's time to have a phone chat with your dad," an insight that came through both clear and true.

Delighted, I asked Carolina to count herself up from 0 to 5 and out of hypnosis.

"Do you remember what you just said as Life Coach Carolina?" I asked after we had switched our seats back.

"Yes, I do."

"That was the missing piece, wasn't it?" I asked. Carolina beamed. I knew then that she would be willing to practice self-hypnosis just one more time.

Carolina quickly slipped herself into a state of trance. "Dive into the darkness, within you or without. Every step of the way, my voice will be there with you," I guided and assured her. Carolina was silent as she courageously dove into the darkness; it was pitch dark and cave-like. Hesitating at the cave entrance to adjust her eyes to the inky blackness, Carolina slowly stepped inside. Unable to see clearly in the dark, she sensed movement and shadows and a tall, feminine presence near her side. It was the dark presence that so successfully filled her with fear. She walked further into the silent cave, the looming presence trailing behind her. With Carolina's senses recalibrated to the quiet and dark, a scene began to solidify around her, voices and images colouring the shape of the darkness.

"I'm feeling claustrophobic, crowded," Carolina confessed. "The shadows are on top of me. They're raising their arms, making me feel that I am… inside… like they are suffocating me. And *she* is *instructing* the crowd," Carolina continued, annoyed with the presence.

"The crowd, are they men or women?"

"Both. But they are more like shadowy spirits. They aren't actually physical or solid like me."

"The shadows are not physical, and with them on top of you, it makes you wonder what you have done to deserve this, doesn't it?"

"I just want them to go away," she replied firmly and confidently.

I needed to learn more about the reasons behind what Carolina was witnessing and experiencing, "Since they are given instructions from the presence, does she want them to go away, too?"

"No. She doesn't."

"She must have a reason. We need to understand why she does not want them to leave you alone. I want you to connect with your inner knowing. From there, allow yourself to *know* who she is and what you have done to deserve this. And why she is doing this to you and not anyone else."

"I was supposed to do something and that I didn't do? And this might be like a punishment?" came Carolina's tremulous admission.

"Speak to the presence directly now and ask, 'What was it that I was supposed to do that I did not do?'"

"…acknowledge her?" Carolina seemed to be taken aback by what came to her awareness.

"So, you have not acknowledged her. Fair enough. We can do that now. But we do not even know who she is, nor what she has done that deserves acknowledgement. How can we acknowledge that which we do not know? Invite her to introduce herself so we might know what we are acknowledging."

"I—" Carolina began, stopped herself, and swallowed hard, searching for some clarity in the vision. "I see a cemetery. I sense she passed away a long time ago. If that makes sense?" So far, nothing about this scene made much sense, but my work frequently traverses through the inexplicable. And in that sense, it did make perfect sense.

Giving it my best sense-making attempt, I kept the stalled Carolina talking, "A cemetery. Did you know her and not acknowledge her death? Did you accidentally step on her grave when you were younger? Is that what you need to acknowledge?"

Carolina corrected me, "I feel like my failure wasn't in *this* life."

"Okay. She wants you to acknowledge her, and she is helping you right now to go all the way to that moment in that life when she passed away."

Carolina was Barbara, a young woman in her late twenties in the 17th century. Barbara stood crammed into a town square; the crowd gathered around a woman bound to a thick, roughly hewn stake. Barbara knew the woman, though she dared not admit it. The woman was her mentor and friend, Mati. And the two lived, worked, and learned together. In her mid-thirties, Mati was a self-taught herbalist and scientist with an aptitude for mixing medicines. Barbara possessed an impressive ability to locate and understand plant species. Theirs was an intellectual kinship; the two women peacefully expanding their knowledge together, exploring the world of plant-based medicine.

Restrained and awaiting her judgement atop that cruel mound of wood, Mati gazed out across the crowd, seeking her friend, and stared at her expectantly. Uneasily under her gaze, Barbara felt Mati was expecting her to do something, anything. Half the townspeople pitied Mati, while others were too enraged by discovering a "witch" in their midst. An overwhelming sense of helplessness paralyzed Barbara. It was a deep and abiding helplessness, that of hers and her friend. All Barbara could do was stand there and watch, too scared to fight, too frozen to hide.

It was doubtful who was feeling worse, Mati bound helplessly to the stake or Barbara standing powerlessly in the crowd. Overcome with an intensity of emotion, Carolina's eyes welled up, and a torrent of tears began to flow down her face.

Past Life Regression is a beautiful form of therapy. Carolina could process her emotions in that safe space, emotions the numbed Barbara could not afford to express in that dangerous, public place. This is how liminal healing can be allowed to occur.

Letting her emotions run unbridled for a while, I guided Barbara-Carolina through: "At this moment, you are standing there in the crowd, Barbara, watching this. All you can do is to allow yourself to feel deeply, feeling for Mati; feeling your own helplessness and hopelessness; feeling the deepest love and gratitude for her. You did enjoy working with her, didn't you? And you do love her, don't you?"

"Yes."

"You can let her know that it is okay. It is going to be over very soon. She will be free. Send that thought to her, 'Very soon, you will be free.' It's all right. Tell her, 'I would help if I knew how, but I do not. I do not know how.' Allow her to know you are feeling the same powerlessness and helplessness, but it will be over very soon, and she will be free.

"Let her know that she has been a wonderful teacher and great companion. She can let go of this life now. She can let go of all the pain. She can release all her sorrow and fear.

"She has been a great healer. Sometimes not everything can go as we plan, but that does not deny the fact that she, Mati, is so good at what she does. Yes, let yourself acknowledge her now. You do acknowledge her, don't you? Acknowledging all she is and all she has been."

Carolina's tears abated gradually, and she began to quiet herself as Barbara carried on her acknowledgments. It was time to move on, so I brought that traumatic scene to an end: "Now, Barbara, allow yourself to know what life is like for you after this. Will you be able to continue your work? Or do you stop?"

"I stopped. I took care of people, but in a different way."

"How were you doing emotionally after Mati was gone?"

"I felt empty and lonely. A little guilty, too. But I kind of accepted it. I guess I receded into myself."

"Okay. Now allow yourself to access the entirety of your soul's journey and its incarnations. After you have done that, does Mati ever come back and reincarnate herself?"

"No, I don't think so."

Instead, Mati had become a haunting ghost, the darkness present in Carolina's life. *Now* it all made sense, Carolina's fear of darkness; her hopelessness in being seen by others; her embarrassment and shame.

Even with Barbara's acknowledgment, I still sensed Mati had some unfinished business. She harboured a good deal of resentment and could benefit from being coached. "Let us go back now," I suggested to Carolina-Barbara, "to that dark, cave-like space. Mati's ghost is there on your right-hand side, slightly taller than you, causing the crowd to confine you. Let her know that we are here to acknowledge her presence. Does she have anything to say at this moment?"

"No. But, I can see she is still processing. She's calmer now, though."

I knew that Carolina was finishing her practicum as a life coach, and I mused whether coaching a ghost might count towards Carolina's practicum hours? Regardless, it would be good practice: "If you were the best life coach, you could coach ghosts, too. You probably never thought about that before, eh?"

Tearfully, Carolina laughed. I paused for several minutes, giving Carolina more time to collect herself.

"One of the things you can tell Mati is that all that has happened, has happened. Everybody has moved on. And you have moved on, taking on another life, in another time and space. Because she is free now, so too can she. She *has* been free. And yet what is the use of her freedom if she will not let go of the past? Preferring to trade on her freedom, keeping herself bound and tethered; a prisoner of the past? There can be a better choice, and she can make that choice. She can come back and have another life.

"Times have changed now. It is different. Now people respect and acknowledge those who have healing abilities.

"Grudges hold no true value, and she surely cannot realize her own gift if she continues to hold onto a grudge from the past. She has a gift, of course. Back then, in the 17th century, no one would openly acknowledge and recognize her gift— nonetheless, a gift she has.

"Tell her you *know* how to help her now, and you are willing and able to help her now. You have already acknowledged her; that was what she was asking. Is there anything else you can do for her? Let her know you will do it if it's within your ability. But for her, there's a better way to be.

"Today, your tears are the proof that you can feel for her and that you do care. But you have already moved on, and so can she. It is also better timing for you to help each other now as if you are still sisters. Let her know you have missed her. I know she's still processing..."

"But she looks much better now since I've shared this with her," Carolina interrupted to update me on Mati's progress.

"Good. Now share with her what life was like for Barbara after she was gone. You felt so empty and lonely. There was little fulfillment left for you in life. You stopped working with plants completely because together you were a very good team—a sisterhood. So maybe, if she so chooses, she can help you in this life, in some way, shape or form. Together you do good things as a team.

"When she is ready, she can leave that cave behind and again be that shining bright light. The fire burned her body but tell her, 'Nobody can destroy who she truly is.' But I would hazard to guess that she already knows that."

There was a long silence as Carolina tearfully continued to coach Mati and herself. Having already taught her self-hypnosis techniques to practice on her own, I wanted to do a final fear check: "Now that we have explored the darkness and this cave in this session, is it fair to say that when you do your self-hypnosis, there is nowhere that you cannot go?"

"Yeah," Carolina replied with more certainty.

"Good," I said. "You know you can just go there, even if it is just a cave; curiosity is all you need. Next time when you go there, she may meet you, and you can continue to heal together. After all, once upon a time, you were like sisters. And it is good to be together. It is good to acknowledge her, and it can never be too late.

"It is good for her to be helped as well because, after all, she wanted to be helped. And after so much time, now you *are* helping her, knowing that in this session, you have done tremendous work.

"Carolina, you are officially the greatest life coach. Not only can you coach people, your hypnotherapist, and yourself, but you can coach a ghost, too. You cannot help but be who you are."

Carolina was crying and laughing at all she had done and experienced. She was brought out of the trance just as she called her sister out of that cave. I had a feeling Mati would be of great support, in so many different ways, in Carolina's life. Lifetimes later, the sisters were finally reunited in profound and meaningful ways.

On the Run

Convergences of Past and Present

"I feel I already know you," Britney said calmly from her seat on my office couch. We had only just met for less than five minutes, but I knew she had browsed my website extensively before contacting me for a series of hypnotherapy sessions. Britney lived a nomadic lifestyle, a non-resident American who travelled the world teaching English to non-native speakers. It afforded her the easy opportunity of living most of the year outside of the U.S.A. Though American herself, she felt her home was becoming more and more violent, and in recent years, she had tragically lost a brother to gun violence. It was this experience that, in part, had Britney seeking my help with better managing her PTSD.

Britney's presenting issues were fear and anxiety, yet the woman who sat before me was calm, composed, and mature. Natural, peaceful energy surrounded Britney, so much so that I found my breathing harmonized into a steady rhythm, and my thoughts were crystal clear. No matter how she described the angst of her inner turmoil, sitting and getting to know Britney was a peaceful and enjoyable experience.

Britney recently finished a teaching job in Spain and was waiting for a new contract to begin in Thailand. To avoid losing her U.S. non-residency status, she had decided upon Vancouver, Canada, as her out-of-country-between-jobs place to stay. She had no prior commitments or engagements in Vancouver; it was a rest spot for Britney, a place to seek emotional balance, well-being, and healing. And a place to explore her curiosity in past life regression and future life progression.

Working with Britney, I quickly discovered she possessed an innate skill for accessing whatever information she needed in the moment; she was a highly intuitive and artistic woman who fully trusted her abilities. Together, these qualities proved to make Britney a hypnotherapist's dream. It did not take her long to be ready to explore and reap the benefits of doing a past life regression. By our second session, she was already reporting feeling safer, relieved from her anxiety, and more secure in her being. If Britney could view a lifetime from which she might better understand her soul's purpose and journey, it could anchor her new sense of safety and security. And that she might carry these feelings with her to her new teaching position and on her continued world travels.

I asked Britney if she had any questions for me before we started the regression.

Feigning seriousness, Britney sat up straight and exclaimed, "Indeed, I do! Is it possible to be reincarnated as an animal?"

"My work has shown me that it is possible. I have regressed people to when they were a polar bear, a dolphin, and other animals. Some even recalled being trees."

Britney looked at me with eyes bright and wide, "I think impatient people need to be reincarnated as trees."

I wanted to laugh but stopped myself, unsure whether Britney was joking or not. She appeared to look rather serious. "Maybe people who are glued to couches watching TV had many lives as trees," I speculated. Britney's seriousness finally broke at that supposition, and we both shared a good laugh.

"I'll tell you why I asked that question," Britney said after we'd collected ourselves again. "On the day of my brother's funeral, a butterfly kept fluttering around me. The whole day. And I've often wondered since if that butterfly was actually my brother reincarnated."

It is not uncommon for me to employ mental confusion, time and spatial distortion techniques to transition a client disengaging from their present reality into a past life reality. However, none of those maneuvers were necessary for Britney. She moved faster than I could verbally guide her during the induction and had to remind herself to keep coming back to the sound of my voice. I had not yet finished guiding her to find a lifetime that could help Britney understand her anxiety, fear, and purpose. However, two different lifetimes had already presented themselves into her awareness. But when we eventually entered the intended lifetime, Britney was hugely surprised. What came to her awareness was nothing like the two lives she had earlier envisioned.

Ashna was lost and lonely, wandering around a hot, humid jungle. His skin was sticky with sweat where his animal skin clothing touched his waist and thighs, his bare feet itchy and wet as they pressed into the damp earth. Standing still, at a loss, Ashna could not decide what to do next or how to find his three friends who were with him earlier. Amidst the humdrum of their babble, Ashna had wandered off, losing his bearings along the way.

Taking some time to rest and re-orient, Ashna finally realized the way back to his sanctuary, a cave of his own that he went to when he needed time alone. From the quiet space of his cave, Ashna moved on, making his way back to his tribe.

The leader of Ashna's tribe believed members of the tribe should all participate equally in the tasks needed to keep the tribe functioning. Ashna disagreed. The young man believed everyone had their own unique talents and ought to be assigned tasks based upon those talents. He felt if people were able to perform these operational tasks based on their skills, it would make for a happier community. Ashna did not dare challenge the chief out of fear of becoming an outcast. Rightly or wrongly, Ashna assumed he needed the tribe for his survival.

Six years later, at the age of thirty-two, Ashna found the courage to speak up about his beliefs; what began as a calm and peaceful discourse with the tribal chief gradually declined into a heated argument. Ashna had hoped his people would hear and support him, but gripped with fear of reprisal from their leader, Ashna took off and fled to his quiet cave and remained there, in self-imposed exile, for a long time. Alone, Ashna's only companion was his fear. Ashna remained fearful and anxiously vigilant about being found by his tribespeople or being discovered by a nearby tribe. Ironically, his fear of being killed by that neighbouring tribe was the foundation for Ashna's fear of becoming an outcast from his own tribe.

After gathering firewood near his hiding place one day, Ashna returned to his cave to find his belongings displaced. He knew that his sanctuary had been discovered and again decided to flee. With no place else to go, Ashna became nomadic: by day, foraging wild berries, plants, and bugs for food, and by night finding a new spot to sleep. He never spent more than two nights in the same place. Ashna's wanderings eventually brought him to a languishing river bordering a lush forest. Ashna crossed the river and entered the forest, searching for food to eat. Hungry and disoriented, he stumbled around in a weakened daze but found no food. He continued walking around aimlessly until the familiar sounds of the river were again audible. Ashna made his way back to the river only to discover it deeper than before; its current too swift to cross. Feeling hopeless, exhausted, and depressed, Ashna dropped to the ground and sat by the river's edge wishing his misery would finally end. He sat, sullen and forlorn, for a long time before he stood up, stepped into the rushing river, and let the current whisk him away.

Upon his death, I guided the spirit to see what had become of his tribe: the old chief had died and leaderless, his tribe had gone in search of Ashna. They remembered he had been the only one who had been brave enough to challenge the old chief. They remembered that Ashna had had a plan for a new and better future for his people, and they wanted *him* to become their new chief. His tribespeople's search had led them to Ashna cave, a discovery that had sent a panic-stricken Ashna on the run and away from stepping into his true purpose.

That life gave Britney a clarifying perspective, one from which she could easily see the parallels between her past and present Self. The modern-day Britney still felt the same opaque fear as the Ashna of old and had taken the same fear-based action: running away. Britney took some time, in that moment of pristine clarity, to integrate all she had learned about her fear, anxiety and emotional responses. With relief, she knew that soon she would stop running and move forward to uncover her true life purpose.

After a Future Life Progression session, I was heartened to learn that after a few more years of travelling and teaching English abroad, Britney would return to North America to settle peacefully in the backcountry of British Columbia and establish a leadership camp for youth.

Just Do It

Probable Past Lives

People who have experienced a past life regression often wonder if what they have experienced was real. Every moment during the regression experience can *feel* real: they can smell, touch, taste, hear, see, and feel the difficult or impossible choices that they made in the moment. Yet, looking back with perspicacity at a regression's end, they can see different choices they could have made, leaving one wondering: *Where might those other choices have taken me on that life path?*

Other therapists may disagree, but I genuinely believe there is a power in PLR Therapy to tap into those alternative lives where potentials are perceived. Does it not seem possible that that same soul made those choices and lived that alternate life path in a parallel timeline? All humans go through this selection process of choosing the right or the best route to take when making decisions. We imagine the possible outcomes of each action *before* deciding upon a particular course of action. And in the journey of living our lives, full of countless decisions, we implicitly develop a set of beliefs and limitations that we come to think of as the components of what it is to be "me."

Susan Watkins talks about this process in her ground-breaking books. In *Conversations with Seth, Book Two*, she introduces the reader to a spiritual entity named Seth as channelled by Jane Roberts. Seth presents the subconscious human process of "remembering" some traits and characteristics over others and then attaching ego to those remembered traits. Thus, defining our distinctive expression of personal identity. And in the background, those other indiscernible traits create a myriad of possible egos that may manifest themselves and give rise to their potential in other probable realities.

There can be a great benefit to clients when they regress to a past life, see and feel the consequences of their choices, have the option to contemplate a parallel reality where they have made different choices, and then visualize how that probable "past life" would turn out.

My observation is that a Parallel Reality Past Life Regression or a Probable Reality Past Life Regression feels as real as any other past life regression, or any other lived experience. It is not simply wishful thinking. By allowing clients to visualize how decisions impact outcomes in past lives, I can better support them in making more informed choices about their current lives.

Jade vividly illustrated this observation. She had emigrated from Panama, married a Canadian and settled in British Columbia, where she was starting a photography business. Though very passionate about her new business venture, Jade was also scared of failing *and* succeeding. Her goal of owning her own business intimidated her. Desiring to move forward without fear, she came to see me for help using Past Life Regression Therapy.

Nathaniel had a passion for poetry and, perhaps, a poetic routine. Every day, the young man walked down to the city square, sat in his favourite spot (the one that had the best lighting), wrote his poems and watched the people come and go, hurrying to or strolling from some destination. When the daylight faded and he could no longer comfortably write,

Nathaniel would amble over to his local pub to meet his friends (and moon over the pretty barmaid he dared not express his feelings to) and show his chums his latest manuscripts. Though written with considerable passion and gusto, no one, friend or foe, paid much mind to Nathaniel's poetry.

Year after year, Nathaniel's routine stayed the same and decade after decade, the results, too, remained the same: nobody expressed a care for his craft or bothered to read his poetry. Disinterest can wear a man down, and with time, Nathaniel began to doubt the merit of his work. He surrendered himself to a deep and despairing depression. Believing there was no value in the thing he loved most in life, he gave up on life and endured his days in the scant cocoon of his bed.

I realized that there was no point in moving forward in this life. It was the eighteenth century, and Nathaniel was already in his fifties. He would likely die the same way he had lived: lonely, defeated, and depressed. I decided to have Nathaniel consider and realize a different probable reality for himself.

"You are lying in bed. Where are your poems, Nathaniel? The manuscripts? Are they around your house?" I asked.

He took his time answering as if he was looking around for the writings. Then replied, "Aye. They are there... in the corner... But nobody cares. I do not care."

"Why don't you go over to the corner and gather your poems together? Then tell me how big or thick a stack you have."

"Oh," came Nathaniel's feeble attempt at surprise, and a little later, "Quite thick. There is a great deal of them." This time, Nathaniel's surprise at the sheer size of his stack of poems was more robust.

"So thick they can be made into a book? Is that right?"

"Aye... Very thick," he acknowledged.

"Have you thought about publishing them?"

"What's the point? Nobody is going to be interested in it! Nobody at all! Who's going to read it? It's worthless. Just worthless."

"How do you know? You haven't tried to present them to a bigger audience. You have shown your poems to a happenstance audience, but you have not sought an audience that may truly appreciate them. Sometimes the people around us are just not our audience, and we need to go past *them* to discover our true audience. Now Nathaniel, if you are to seek a way to have them published, where would you take them? What's the first step that you can take?"

Nathaniel paused, thinking, and then hesitatingly replied, "I guess I can take them to the church."

"All right. You've been lying in bed. And it seems there is nothing better you can think of doing at the moment. Today, I want you to take this manuscript to the church. Don't worry about the outcome because you don't care about the manuscript anyway. You might as well just take it to the church and have them look at it."

That stumped him. He could not think of a single way to argue with me.

"Okay," Nathaniel conceded.

"Before you go…do you have a mirror at home?"

"Aye."

"Then go and look at yourself in the mirror. How do you look?"

"Not good," he responded with surprised disappointment, "I look shite. My hair and beard are long and unkempt. And my clothes are due a wash and change."

"Do you have something more presentable to wear?"

"Aye, I do. A white, cotton shirt."

"Go ahead, change into that white shirt and a nicer pair of pants. You may need to splash some water on your face, shave and trim your hair before you take your manuscript to the church."

Dutifully, Nathaniel went and readied himself for the outing. When he finished dressing, I had him view himself in the mirror again.

"…better," he almost smiled.

"All right. Get your manuscript together and take it to the church." I paused for a moment to allow Nathaniel to see himself going to the church. "Now you are at the church. What do they say?"

"They take the manuscript and tell me to come back for it in one week."

Feeling a renewed sense of accomplishment after delivering his manuscript of poems to the church, Nathaniel, ever a creature of habit, went back to his old haunt, the local pub. Something was different as Nathaniel walked into the sour, musky warmth of the pub. The pretty waitress paid him more attention, lingering longer than necessary, inventing excuses to serve or talk to him.

A week later, Nathaniel returned to the church for his manuscript.

"What do they say about your manuscript?" I asked.

Nathaniel paused. Jade burst into tears. "Oh, no, no… They are going to publish it! They like it! They are going to publish it. I can't believe it!" Overwhelming relief, joy, wonder, and surprise poured down Jade's face in those tears.

Patiently I waited until Jade could collect herself, and then I moved Nathaniel forward in time: his book, written with so much love and dedication and passion, once published, was a huge success. The public loved it, and Nathaniel became a famous writer who married that pretty barmaid.

I asked the now-famous poet if a girl from his future came to visit him and was to ask him for his advice on her new photography business, what would he tell her?

Nathaniel-Jade again burst into tears. Nathaniel knew precisely to whom I was referring, and he began to speak with Jade directly: "Do it! *Just do it!* Show it to the world. Do not worry about how it is going to be received or how others might look at you. Just do it! You have so much talent to express and passion to share. Everything will sort itself out. Just do it; move forward in your life and put yourself out there in the world."

With that, I brought Jade back and out of hypnosis.

Two months after our session, I received an invitation from Jade. She was hosting an exhibition showcasing her photography. The invitation read: "...You are cordially invited to **Passion and Promise: A Photographic Journey of Possible Realities by visual story-teller Jade.**"

Seer's Plight

Lessons from Parallel Realites

Right from the beginning, I noticed the parallels within Samantha: by profession, she was a radio announcer, yet her spirit, she shared, was preparing her to become a channeler. She was confident in her ability and said it felt natural and that she was pretty good at it. "When I was little before my sister was born, I would play and talk to my invisible friends," Samantha continued. "A little old lady, a little boy and a little girl." I thought how interesting this must make her journey, first being a radio announcer and then discovering that she *is* the radio.

I was doing Parts Therapy to help Samantha with her presenting anxiety issue. It was then, in our first hypnotherapy session together, that a robust part interrupted us. Samantha called this part "Spirit." Eager, and seeing an opportunity to come through while Samantha was in a trance, Spirit seized the moment to deliver her a message: "It is time for Samantha to start doing channelling. She has been putting up too many barriers in the form of distractions and has lost herself in them. If she continues to block herself, it is going to take a bolt of lightning to crack her open!"

I asked Spirit to enlighten us and give us a little more information. Spirit answered my request by taking us to a past life of Samantha's: William was only seven years old, and he, his mother and his younger brother were being hunted like a rabbit chased by hounds. The little family darted and ran through the forest, trying to put some distance between them and their pursuers. Desperate to save her children, their mother realized their best chance of escaping would be to split up—William with his brother and her on her own. In due course, their mother was caught. But William and his brother survived by hiding in the forest until it grew dark.

Frightened and alone, the boys were lost, not knowing what to do or where to go without their mother. The younger boy began to cry. William, too, wanted to cry but thought it better to appear strong for his little brother. The dark forest grew even darker, the shadows of the trees loomed ominously, and every crack of a twig and rustling of the leaves sounded like a threat. Just then, on the edge of panic, the moon rose, full and bright, and the brothers could begin to make sense of the shapes in the dark. They scrambled through the underbrush and came upon a path leading to a swiftly flowing river. They knew the river. Their village was near this river, although much farther upstream. The boys had crossed that river many times before and decided to cross it again to make their way back.

Downstream the river was much deeper than the boys had imagined, with the water almost reaching their chests. They waded slowly towards the middle, where the current was strongest; William's brother tripped, his small foot caught between submerged rocks. Desperately big brother tried to free little brother, but the current was too strong, the river too deep, and the young boy drowned.

William was devastated; first, his mother was captured and presumed dead, and now he'd lost his little brother to a raging river because he was too small to save him. Amidst his grief, the young boy realized he still had to keep moving and find shelter. Near his village, William found a cabin and hid underneath it, safe and out of sight. He hid there for almost a year. The area was familiar to William, and the house provided sufficient shelter and was a convenient place from which to steal food.

Curious and a little impressed, I asked William what he did underneath that cabin all that time. "Shh…" Samantha put a finger to her lips, as if the boy was afraid that the hypnotherapist's voice would disturb those people living in the house and thus reveal to them his hiding place. "I talk to my invisible friends," the boy whispered. "There is an old lady, a boy, and a girl."

Missing food and a young boy talking to himself beneath the floorboards eventually drew unwanted attention, and William was caught and arrested. A jailed, frightened eight-year-old William learned that he would be in service to the king when he came of age. During his imprisonment, William became increasingly aware that people thought him uniquely strange, like his mother, who was rumoured to be a powerful witch. For thirteen long, hard years, William braved prison, his only friends, spirits from the spirit world.

When William turned twenty-one, he was released and brought before the king. The king demanded that William predict the war patterns of his enemies to know what neighbouring regions were thinking before they had even planned it. William knew that being a great seer was part of his heritage, a birthright typically associated with the females of his bloodline.

Turning to me, William asked me as an observer of life, "But I'm male. Men cannot be witches, can they?" Aside from the spirits, it seemed I was the only person with whom William could safely express his doubts. But he was in front of the king, and William could see no other choice. Holding himself still and focused, William closed his eyes and opened himself up as a conduit to other realms. He knew he could speak to spirits and thought to himself, *Perhaps, I can just ask the spirits, and they will tell me the answer for the king.*

He sat perfectly still with his eyes closed for quite some time. Then something almost imperceptible to the king shifted in William's being, and he began to recite what he had received. "An army is coming," he said, concentrating and pausing. "From the east. An army is coming from the east. They will be at our gates in a fortnight, and we will not win the battle."

The king's worst fear manifested. In a fit of powerless rage, he ordered his guards to throw William off the highest castle tower.

Arriving at the moment of death, I guided the spirit to look back at William's life and asked, "Is there any unfinished business?"

"I wish I had told my mother how much I loved her," the spirit paused, then realized, "I was not true to myself in this life. I *am* a seer. It is the heritage of my family. But I wasted so many years hiding and waiting in fear. What a waste of life!"

"Knowing what you now know, if you could do it again, would you do anything differently?"

"I would not deny it. I would just *be* it."

"How did you deny it?"

"I hid under that cabin for a year," William's spirit sneered at his incarnate self.

"Instead of hiding beneath that cabin, what else could you have done?"

"I could have lived my life as a seer. And I could have told anyone who wanted to know what the spirits showed me."

"Would you tell people in the same village? Or in a different village?"

"All over the world."

"Would that make a difference? They would put you in jail anyway."

"I know. But that is my point: I was *meant* to spread the message! And I did not!"

"As a seven-year-old boy, you did not know any better. Without a mother or family, you did your best to protect yourself and survive. Now looking back as a twenty-one-year-old man, even though you know by choosing to be who you truly are, you would not impact the outcome. You would still die at the same young age, but you may have made a difference—"

"—To the world, and to my soul," William's spirit interrupted, eagerly agreeing.

I spoke directly to the soul, then: "There was, indeed, a plan for that life. Yet, being so young and unwise, William allowed his fear to consume him…"

Again, his Soul-self interrupted me, "William's mother was *meant* to leave her young boys alone in the forest. Her work was complete, and her journey was done. This created the space for William to embrace his birthright and let his people know that he was now the new seer of that region.

"Many people became lost because William did not speak up and claim what was his. Other people's lives could have been saved or have been totally different. William's staunch denial of his true self caused a chain of suffering. Rather than sharing his gift of sight from a place of free agency, William only delivered his message when *forced* to do so.

"That life as William has established a framework of failure for many of my other lifetimes. It created a subconscious pattern of not owning the gift. It created an illusion of safety and ingrained a pattern of *hiding* the gift, of not accepting who I truly am."

I had an idea, "All right, in today's work, let us take a look at the life of William in another probable parallel reality. Let us go back in time.

"When I count from 5 to 1, go back to that forest again. Go back to when your mother left you and your little brother. You are just seven, again."

There, in that moment of splitting from an old reality to the new, William told his mother just how much he loved her and recalled his mother's parting words: "Follow the river back to the village, Will. But stay on this side. Do *not* try to cross here. It isn't safe." She hugged her boys fiercely and whispered in William's ear, "Find somewhere safe where you can leave your little brother. It will be hard, but you must not go back for him. You must make the rest of your journey alone."

Tearfully, William did as his mother had told him to do and left his little brother tucked safely at the edge of the forest where passersby would see him. He hoped that someone would be compassionate enough to take the small boy in and care for him.

As he left his brother, he was careful not to cry until the younger boy could no longer see him. When his emotions subsided, he returned to their village, telling anyone he met that his mother was gone, that she had entrusted him with the gift, and he would now be the one delivering messages for them.

Years later, William would tell his people about the coming war. He encouraged them to leave their homes and the area when the time came and go across the border to the south, where they could find refuge.

William came to realize that the greatest gift he brought to his village was the example he set for other seers who were, as yet, not embracing their abilities. People came from all around to seek William for healing and spiritual guidance. Consciously, he did not know how to help them, but he allowed his gifts to flow through him to comfort, counsel, and heal. His life and role in the community served as an example for others like him to step forward, embrace their gifts, and be accepted. He felt good to be the person he was born to be.

The king eventually learned of his powerful gifts, and in his sixteenth year, William was locked up and imprisoned. The king coveted William's ability and desired him all to himself. Life from that moment onward closely mirrored William's parallel reality of before. The only difference was that the king did not wait to monopolize William's gifts.

When William turned twenty-one, the king asked the same question he had asked in that other parallel reality, and William still told him of the coming invasion. The message that William had told his fellow villagers years earlier. The end was still the same for William, though. The king flew into a violent rage and ordered William be put to death.

At the top of the castle, from its highest tower, William looked back at this parallel reality life and knew he had done well. It felt good and right to have lived how he had chosen to live and done what he was born to do. He realized that doing what he was born to do was no more onerous than deciding not to do it, but it was far more meaningful.

The soul spoke from that broader sense of awareness the afterlife affords. It confirmed Samantha was destined to be a seer in this life, just like William had been in the past. But to become who she was meant to be, Samantha needed to let go of her ego.

Ever the seer, the soul predicted there would be a baby boy born to Samantha within the next two years, and things would change rapidly for her after she had given birth. The baby would serve to open a channel for Samantha, and that boy would be the reincarnation of William's younger brother.

The soul brought its message to an end, "When you understand that time does not exist as you think it does, and you put that together with the idea that your point of power is ever in the present, then you will not feel at the mercy of things that occurred with past personalities. You will see and know that your reality is now. And from that reality, a multitude of probabilities and possibilities are cast outward like seeds on the wind."

More than a year after my session with Samantha, I strolled along Vancouver's oceanside walkway, the Seawall at English Bay. It was a balmy summer's evening, the kind that seems to linger comfortably and only toys with the idea of night. Behind me was a group of happily chatty people. I was enjoying the views at my usual leisurely pace, and I moved aside to allow them to pass. I caught a glimpse of a woman joyfully sporting a rounded belly. She was laughing, holding hands with her partner. I smiled to myself; it was good to see Samantha following her path.

Free to Be

The Magic Within

I have helped clients journey to their past lives almost daily for more than a decade. Rarely am I surprised when a client turns out to be royalty or somebody notable. Kristy was neither famous nor royal in her past life, yet her story captivated me. What that life lacked in celebrities, it made up for in surprising, dramatic plot twists that constantly snaked and pivoted whenever the story seemed to be coming to a natural conclusion.

Although she had a wonderful partner, Kristy felt inadequate in her relationship. She struggled with a relentless "hang-up," a restless anxiety about her boyfriend's ex-wife. Feelings of alienation and exclusion plagued Kristy. She believed others rarely saw any value in her point of view. Her feelings of inadequacy would bubble over at times, engulfing her in an overwhelming sense of hopelessness. One day, the whisper of salvation came when Kristy was listening to a Hay House Radio interview with past life regressionists. Kristy decided to shake free of the iron grip those emotions had on her right then and there. She would have a past life regression! I was happy to assist Kristy with her healing. Using the exact words that she had used to describe her feelings, I bridged her back into her timeline as Anton.

Candlelight flickered and warmed the edges of the shadows. It was dark inside the small house where a lonely baby Anton stood in his crib, watching his older brothers Franz and Nikolaus playing, heedless of his desire to join them. The three boys lived by themselves in that little house in Austria, far away from the prying eyes of neighbours and the parental concerns of responsible adults.

Feared to be witches who wielded powerful magic through dark spells, zealous townsfolk from the nearest town had dragged the boys' parents from their home and burnt them alive at the stake. In the swift succession of his birth, young Anton was both motherless and fatherless, bearing no memory of those who had lovingly brought him into the world. The townspeople were uncertain what to do about the three brothers; dogma passionately implied that the children of devil-workers were dangerous and ought to be put to death to protect the purity of others. Yet, individual morals offered that the boys were innocents needing care. The matter resolved itself when a townswoman stepped forward to act as guardian ad litem for Franz, Nikolaus, and Anton. Karoline hiked out of town every day to Anton's cabin to cook for him and his brothers and tend to their most basic needs.

Notwithstanding the kindness, Karoline's role in Anton's life was rudimentarily custodial. And the three-year-old was often left in his crib unattended. Anton cried hard and cried relentlessly. Try as he might to follow his brothers everywhere they went, he could not keep up; the boys were older and stronger and could easily outpace him. Franz and Nikolaus felt Anton was simply too small, young, and delicate to join in their fun and adventures. Forbidden from ever journeying into town, Franz and Niko would hunt and play and forage in the fields and woods by their home.

Sequestered to his home, Anton mostly spent his days alone. He grew up never engaging with other children save his brothers or with an adult, with the brief exception of

Karoline's daily and chiefly wordless appearances. Niko and Franz and that little cabin were Anton's entire world. Living and growing up in such a strangely isolated environment, Anton did not utter a single word until he was almost seven years old. When one day, feeling particularly hungry, he asked for a second helping of food. The older boys dumbly stared at their younger brother for several minutes before meeting his request, then continued as if nothing extraordinary had just occurred.

Six years later, Franz and Nikolaus decided it was time for them to leave home. Hoping for a chance at a more normal life, the older brothers planned to move far away from where anyone might know of them or their parents. Freedom was risky; they would undoubtedly be persecuted if they got caught. Their decision was an easy one; they had been excluding Anton from their private club his whole life and decided to leave him behind, once again and for the last time. They reasoned that bringing Anton along would certainly increase their odds of getting captured. Anton begged and pleaded with his brothers to take him with them, but the brothers would not budge in their resolve.

The night of Franz and Nikolaus's escape felt like the longest night of Anton's little life. The devastating loneliness felt so final, so infinite, he thought he might never know anything else. Dutifully, Karoline arrived the following morning to cook the boys' meals, and what she found shocked her: wet from tears, urine and sweat was a bound Anton, tied to the old, rot-blackened kitchen table. "I'm the small one," the thirteen-year-old Anton responded to Karoline's bewildered query, "So I just obeyed. I let them tie me up."

Anton lived in utter solitude with his brothers gone, and the next ten years of his life passed by with almost no interruption from the outside world. Karoline, upset by how Nikolaus and Franz had left Anton, and gravely disapproving of their deception, ceased coming to the cottage to cook his meals. Steeped in a deep sadness, Anton longed for his brothers. He wondered whether their escape had been successful or if they were even alive. Wonder and yearn as he might, Anton never saw his two brothers again.

He kept on with his daily routine, working in the fields day and night, blending the herbs he grew into tonics, balms, and elixirs. And on the occasions when his loneliness was at its greatest, Anton conversed with the animals. Several years after his brothers' departure, Karoline returned with a proposal for Anton, a goods exchange with the townsfolk: Anton would spirit out to the edge of town and fill the herbal remedy stockpiles of a secret trading post, where some of the townspeople knew to receive them. They would then leave him offerings there, in thanks and trade, necessities that Anton could not grow himself. The transactions were entirely faceless, contactless. Anton never saw who came in need of his medicines nor who left the things he required to continue surviving on his own.

The monotony of Anton's days bled one into another, varied only by the changing seasons; there was no joy, only longing. *That's it*, I thought. *The whole of Anton's sad and lonely life wouldn't be any different. This might even be a short life.* I could easily see how Kristy's unsettling feelings of inadequacy, hopelessness, and alienation had branches that extended far back into Anton's life and, in fact, were rooted there.

I asked Anton to move forward in time to the next significant event of his life, half-expecting it to be the moment of his death: again, it was dark. Yet, he was not alone. A twenty-eight-year-old Anton stood amidst a group of people in a large, underground chamber; musty and secluded, the cavern held the air of a secret meeting place. Flames leapt and crackled from burning torches, casting strange and lively shadows that danced across the chamber's ceiling and walls. People from the town and neighbouring towns had brought him to this place. Anton sensed someone needed him for the first time in his uneventful life. He knew his presence in this concealed place directly resulted from his furtive trades with the townspeople over the many years since his brothers left.

Those gathered around the young man believed he possessed a magical power to heal. Like his parents before him, they thought him capable of great magic, that he could see what others could not. Unlike his parents, the people did not wish to harm Anton but were most anxious for him to start performing his healing magic on them and their loved ones.

Fearful and confused, Anton nervously inched back towards the cavern wall; he believed himself to be nothing more than a simple farmer with no magic to share. *This may be his death scene, after all,* I thought. *The people will grow tired of him professing his lack of magic and, in anger, kill him.* Once again, I thought I knew the course of things.

Slowly, the group that surrounded Anton began to convince him that he did, indeed, bear magical powers. Eagerly, they showed him clippings of herbs they had gathered for him after watching him working alone in his fields. They shared tale after tale with him about how his traded concoctions held the power to heal those who used them. Anton did have magic, a healing magic and intuitive knowledge of the earth. And he *was* already sharing it and being earnestly invited to share it even more.

Anton returned to that cavern often after that. It became The Healing Chamber, a place where the sick and unwell were brought before Anton. Becoming increasingly more comfortable with his newly assigned role, Anton began to let his creativity loose, devising elaborate rituals to administer his assortment of treatments and medicines. The unofficial council that had first brought Anton to the cave treated him well, and he began to enjoy his moments with them. Anton remained active working in his fields when he wasn't busy treating people in The Healing Chamber. He learned, and he grew. His natural ability with plant identification deepened, with intuition giving way to mastery and the evolution of better, more complex tinctures and potions to heal his people's ailments.

Anton grew closer to the people, and some began believing that his magic was powerful enough that Anton possessed the ability to *see* the truth and consequences of future events. It was unclear if he believed it or was just going along to get along. Nevertheless, *I* was convinced. I asked Anton to use his ability of sight to see if his brothers were still alive. He felt that they were but that they were also very far away.

Anton spent a happy and purposeful seven years living this better life until his arcane healing rituals drew the harsh and unwanted attention of the regional authorities. He was arrested and sent to prison, charged with the unlawful practicing of magic and witchcraft. The laws had not changed in his favour since his parents' time.

Though prison life was gruelling and hellishly cold, Anton expressed no regrets, "I did not go with my brothers. I stayed and made my own choices, took my own risks. It was worth it. I learned skills; I made meaningful connections. I changed my life for the better, and in so doing, I saved the life of many people." *Now that was finally it,* I thought. *Anton would spend the rest of his life in prison.*

I moved him forward to the next significant event of his life: It was three years later, and although still in prison, a war had broken out in his homeland. Anton, along with his fellow prisoners, were each given a sword and sent off to strengthen the efforts on the frontline. *Ironic, a healer becoming a fighter. And could this be the end then?* I wondered. *Would Anton survive the war for which he had no training?*

One evening, as Anton prepared the troops' meal bubbling unpleasantly over the fire, he added a healthy dose of "seasoning" to the dinner pot. He'd discovered and collected some powerful soporific herbs during their routine nightly patrols. That night, all the soldiers and army commanders fell into a long, deep, restful sleep while Anton stole away under the cover of darkness.

He lost count of the days and nights as he skittered through small towns, always moving away from the war, like a man hunted until he arrived at a village where no one had heard of where he was from or its war. Anton found work as a farmhand on one of the village's family farms and settled into a simple, honest life there. But the most exciting thing about this new chapter in life was the *freedom*. His new home felt worlds away from where he had previously lived. No one there knew of his parents, abilities, or imprisonment. "I don't need to live in hiding anymore!" he exclaimed. It was a happy life, full of love. Anton married and had a daughter in that village that had become his Eden and continued, on occasion, to blend the wild herbs that grew naturally in the forests and fields near his home.

More than two hours had passed in our session: Anton's life had taken many unexpected and eventful turns; I had thought we were at the end multiple times. Yet, Anton's life went on in new and different ways.

Anton was an older man of fifty-eight years when he became ill with a great fever and chills. The colour drained from his face, and with his last breath, he thought, "I made it! I had a real-life." He then passed peacefully, surrounded by the love and warmth of his family and friends.

I brought the regression full circle for Kristy by doing a contextualization[9]. The residual emotions of that past life had become trigger points in Kristy's current-life relationship. So, we re-examined the behaviours of Anton's brothers, Franz and Nikolaus, his reactions to them, and how Kristy's experiences resulted from Anton's thoughts, beliefs, and fears.

"Oh, I sometimes reacted out of such intense and old pain that my boyfriend could not make sense of it! As he has no clue to the wounds from my past life, nor was he even in it," Kristy exclaimed. It was a natural segue for me to ask Kristy if she could identify anyone from Anton's life in her present life. Interestingly enough, she recognized her boyfriend's ex-wife and their young child as Anton's older brothers. *Could Kristy's boyfriend, who was not identified in her life as Anton, symbolize the new life that Anton eventually allowed himself to embrace?* I wondered.

---

[9] By drawing out patterns and motifs that hold influences in a current life, we reinterpret and translate significance events from past or concurrent lives.

All therapists are likely aware of how past wounds and fears can get stuck in our current existence. Anton finally made it to a life of love, freedom, and acceptance. However, coming into a new lifetime as Kristy, those uncleared and as yet not fully released blocks and emotions of fear and hopelessness, inadequacy, and alienation, had remained firmly rooted.

Helping Kristy put her entire life of Anton into an unfettered perspective, we went through his whole life story again, and at each turn, I anchored her on a positive emotional state.

The positive repositioning of the process gave rise to a realization: She/Anton felt isolated and alienated because people *knew* them to be powerful, not because they possessed no real value or worth.

Anton's life has been one of the most memorable in my work. Two years after our session, Kristy emailed me to share the next chapter in her life: she married her boyfriend in his homeland, Latvia. And her husband's ex-wife and child had been present at their wedding. Yes, Anton and Kristy, I am sure glad you made it!

Falling to Grace

From Unwanted to Unfettered

In the rich, sapphire blue sky of my professional and personal memories, Minna is the star that shines the brightest. She sparkles like a rare and precious gem, and even her deep, dark eyes sparkle and cast her light. I first met Minna at a networking event. Packed with strangers wearing name badges, I idly wandered around the crowded space, free from the anxiety of remembering strangers' names. It was then that I caught the eye of a dazzling young woman. We quickly started a conversation, engaging in the Q&A that seems typical of professional networking events. I told her I was a hypnotherapist; Minna asked me about Past Life Regression, her keen interest in the subject felt personal. She had already shared her love of stories and gift for storytelling. And just as my interest piqued, someone else entered our orbit, diluting the conversation from getting too deep into the topic. Gradually, I moved on to the next person and the next meet-and-greet.

Minna found me again later, though. She wanted to know if I had lunch plans, as she wished to take me for lunch at Café Artigiano, just down the street from the event space. Away from the networking event, Minna appeared more comfortable with exploring PLR further. What started as a casual lunch swiftly evolved into a client intake consultation. Minna hoped to address the overwhelming anxiety she experienced in many aspects of her life, including her romantic relationships. We set up a hypnotherapy appointment on the spot.

Minna came to the session expressing a burning curiosity about past lives, one that had been with her for a long time. We got to work without further ado.

She was standing outside, deep in the Kirishima Mountains, barefoot save for socks. The sun was gleaming off her simple, loosely flowing white robe. I asked where she slept at night. "I stay in a big wooden house with many rooms," came her reply. "A temple. It is very calm and peaceful there. I have my own bedroom where I sleep on a quilted mattress on the floor."

"Like a futon?" I asked.

"Yes."

"If there are any mirrors in your room, go and take a look at yourself. What do you see?" She indicated there were indeed mirrors in her room and described a young, Asian-looking woman, about seventeen years old. Moving her through the house, I instructed her to go to a typical dinnertime: nine people sat around a long table eating simple fare. She wanted to eat her dinner with her hands but doing so was not permitted. Sitting to her right was a priest, with whom she did not feel completely comfortable. But across the table from her sat her friend, a young man named Kaneto. Kaneto taught beginners' Buddhist courses to the temple visitors.

Minna had transported us to 1806 Kirishima, Japan, and the life of Anieko. I asked Anieko to describe a typical day. She told me she spent much of her time cleaning and training, and in her free time, she enjoyed meeting and speaking with the temple visitors, playing on her own, walking in nature and watching the animals in the nearby mountain forests and valleys.

A priestess in training, Anieko grew up in that big house without any family. The only memory she had was a dim image of her father leaving her in the temple's care when she was three years old. She never saw her father or her family again, and it was the first moment of Anieko's life that she remembered feeling unwanted and abandoned.

Her tutelage in becoming a priestess was a small mercy and primarily served as a distraction from those tenebrous feelings. She was fascinated by the stories and lore that threaded her instruction. Still, Anieko was often late for her training and barely suppressed her defiance while there. She preferred doing things her own way rather than abiding by the temple's rigid formalities and austere rituals.

I asked Anieko to move forward to the next significant moment in her life, where she found herself, at twenty-eight years old, living in a village as a prostitute. At that point, the regression felt a bit like pressing the fast-forward button on one of those old cassette tape players. Minna had overshot her mark and needed to rewind nine years to a nineteen-year-old, Anieko, and the reason for her leaving the temple. She had fallen in love with her childhood friend, Kaneto, and the two had become secret lovers. Their secret love did not long remain hidden, and when discovered, Anieko was excommunicated and cast out of the temple. Being male, and therefore, less evil, or subject to temptations than a woman, the priests had allowed Kaneto to stay. They had invested considerable time, effort, and instruction into the young man. Filled with bitter resentment and despair and a deep anger towards all concerned, Anieko left the only home she had ever known.

Not knowing where to go, Anieko felt utterly lost and alone. I reminded her that she used to like to talk with the visitors at the temple: "Is it possible for you to ask any of them for help?" I suggested.

"No. I am too proud," Anieko replied, though she spoke like one who was ashamed. Sixteen years after her father entrusted her to the temple, this was the second time that Anieko had been left unwanted and abandoned in her short life.

Her increasing sense of being easily expendable and undesirable shadowed her like a haunting spectre while she wandered the genial countryside. Only Anieko's sense of pride kept her moving onward and forward.

Her wanderings eventually brought her to a small village, where a local villager took in a desperately cold and hungry Anieko. The offer of shelter in the crowded residence was neither a show of hospitality nor an act of kindness. It was a brothel whose keepers mistreated Anieko gravely, molesting her person while repeating her worthlessness. The villagers knew what happened in that house. The elder villagers pitied the girl, and her peers lusted after her.

In that village, Anieko lost her freedom more profoundly than ever before. The 'training' to become a prostitute was far less lengthy than becoming a priestess, and it was not long before prostitution became Anieko's way of life.

Tears ran down Minna's face like a mountain rain. She was processing so much pain and intensely raw emotions in such a small window of time.

We pressed the fast forward button on that life once again and found Anieko at eighty-three, long since retired from a life of prostitution. She was living peacefully, alone in a small mountain cabin. The therapist in me was delighted and surprised. Anieko's life had seemed so desperate and filled with pain. I asked for details about Anieko's retired life. I wanted to know more about how she had ended up here, so far removed from the life she had been living before. "My daughter comes to visit me when she is able," Anieko shared. "I am of a great age now," Anieko chuckled lightly. "But I am in good health," she said proudly. "So, my days are filled with walking and spending time tending to my gardens."

"You came to the mountain after you retired?" I asked.

"Yes. And now nobody wants anything from me anymore. No obligations, no demands. Instead of feeling pity for myself, I realized I was finally free. The mountain took me in, and I have made it my home." It made perfect sense; the mountainside, animals, forests, and valleys had been a solace to Anieko in her temple years. Likewise, her earlier Buddhist training brought peace to Anieko in the latter stages of her life. Starting on a mountain, cast down into the valley, and coming home again to the mountain, Anieko's journey of finding grace and redemption had taken her full circle.

She looked back on her life: "It was very unfortunate," was all Anieko would say. Yet, when asked what different choices she might have made in her life, her response was simple and definitive: "None." There was nothing she would have done differently. Alone she had suffered betrayal, loneliness, and abandonment; survived great pain and abuse, and through all that turmoil, had still known love and peace.

Anieko's life-review insights found Minna's face gradually relaxing and brightening, and I asked Anieko if she ever missed Kaneto. Her attention shifted slightly following my question, and she hesitated before replying, "Sometimes." Her answer sparked a connection for Minna. She recognized Kaneto. That same soul was present in her current life. "It's my boyfriend!" Minna whispered through a torrent of tears.

I recalled my lunch-date-cum-consultation with Minna: she'd told me she had experienced a lot of abandonment, and the only person she could trust in her life was her boyfriend. Minna knew that her boyfriend would always be there by her side no matter what happened to her. "I don't even know why. But I can always count on him," she had said.

A thought danced into my awareness, and I imagined it must have been equally challenging on Kaneto emotionally when Anieko left their home at the Kirishima temple. Perhaps at that time, Kaneto had even set a soul commitment to come back again and meet his love, to support and protect her when he had previously been unable.

Anieko died sometime in her late eighties. "Too old to count exactly how old I am," she whispered on her deathbed. Surrounding the elderly Anieko were her loved ones, her daughter and her daughter's family. The door of the little mountain cabin stood open to the fresh mountain air and the brilliance of a sunny day. Peacefully and readily, Anieko drew her last breath.

I asked what her last conscious thought was. Anieko sighed, "I am going to live an average life next time," she answered with a smile. *From Buddhist priestess to village prostitute is a mighty extreme swing,* I mused. *I can certainly understand the desire for an "average" life.*

Free of physical form, her soul told me of the gracefully towering trees it saw. I sensed that in nature is where she always sought her refuge. I remembered how much Anieko loved walking in the mountains and watching the animals while she was living at the temple. Seeing that beautiful setting as an opportunity, I instructed her soul to let go of any residual, heavy emotions, like anxiety and fear, that still burdened it.

It was then that the soul went to the light and met its spirit guide. The guide communicated directly with me through Minna: "Anieko's feelings of abandonment are anchored deep in this soul. That is why Minna feels her anxiety so intensely in this life; it is rooted in Anieko's fear and pain."

I asked the spirit guide to help the soul transmute and broaden the perspective of Anieko's life. The Guide obliged, "The only chance for Anieko to survive as a child was for her father to give her away to the temple. What Anieko saw as abandonment was, in truth, a great act of love. Her father wished so strongly for his baby girl to survive, and 'giving her up' was the only way that she could."

"Is Minna's life the 'average life' that was intended by Anieko?"

"No," the answer suggested that her soul did not entertain such mundane concepts as "average." Minna's guide then told me about her future. She was to become an emotional healer in six- or seven-years' time. Combining her innate ability to feel things deeply and her storytelling prowess, the more life experiences Minna had, the more she would naturally develop her healing gift. And become the caring, kind, and compassionate emotional healer she came here to be.

"The Archangel Michael will be her protector," imparted her Guide. "With whom Minna can speak whenever she needs and pleases. Archangel Michael will help Minna with clearing away any and all delusions she may still have."

Seeing an invitation, I called on Archangel Michael to join us. He willingly came in and added to the Guide's discourse: "In the future, Minna will be fine. For now, she simply needs to breathe and realize that life becomes much harder when you try and do everything by yourself. She does not need to do that. The Universe, her guides, and angels want to help her. She just needs to ask. I am always here to help her when she needs it."

The archangel continued to share that learning to ask for help was one of the big lessons in Minna's life. He pointed to Anieko's life as an example. Her life after leaving the temple might have been quite different if she only put aside her pride and asked for help.

A few days after Minna's regression and life review, I received an affirming email from her. She wrote telling me how hypnotherapy had helped her a great deal in opening up her subconscious. Minna could see things differently and from new perspectives than before: "It has also miraculously allowed me to feel lighter and more collected," she wrote. I felt Minna's story did not only belong to her, though. Could Anieko's noble station as a priestess, despairing fall to prostitution, and subsequent rise to peace, love and grace not be a metaphor for humankind's innocence, falling, rebirth, and ascension?

Ancient Visitations

Travelling Inward to the Light

Fiona came back for her third Past Life Regression session within a month. She had taken a month-long break from being a flight attendant, and as Fiona frequently travelled for her work, she had little desire to do so during her time off. But Fiona did want to travel, just a different kind of travel that carried her inward, and hypnotherapy was the perfect vehicle. Fiona wanted to know who she had been in previous lives. More important than learning about all the different bodies and minds her spirit had inhabited, she wanted to discover who she truly was. And Fiona had dedicated the month for just that purpose. Having scheduled five sessions only four or five days apart, Fiona was ready for the discovery.

In our previous two sessions, Fiona had regressed to two different male lives: a local governor, who died simply by choosing to leave his body, and the unique and curious life of Hoo.

A few feet away from an enormous sabretooth tiger, Hoo stood face to face with the beast, poised to attack. It was hard to determine who was the true predator in this scene: the intent, sure-footed caveman draped in animal skins or the ferocious tiger. For a fleeting second, the sabretooth hesitated in his crouch, and seizing his opportunity, Hoo pounced and deftly slew the animal. Scouring the underbrush, the caveman sought out a sturdy, fallen branch, and when he finally located a suitable one, he methodically secured the animal to it. Hanging upside down, unceremoniously, Hoo hauled his quarry through the jungle and back to his village, where the big game would become food, clothing, tools, and jewellery for his tribe.

He was a skilled and fearless hunter, well-valued by his clan, who loved the thrill of the hunt. But over time, Hoo developed a deep affinity with the animals he encountered, speaking with them heart to heart (though he quite decidedly disliked snakes and lizards), and eventually became friends with an injured tiger he had once hunted. First communicating with the creature to reassure the tiger he was there to help, Hoo knelt on the ground, placed his hands over the tiger's infected wound, and healed it. That tiger was very dear to Hoo, and the caveman often played with the wild cat, showing his affection by safely hugging and nuzzling it.

It was not the first time Hoo had healed someone by laying his hands on them. Whenever his children or their friends hurt themselves, he would tend to their cuts and broken bones by laying his hands on the injured limb.

Befriending the tiger brought the end to Hoo's hunting days. He turned his back on killing and learned to live on the many fruits, nuts, flowers, mosses, and bugs that grew in and around his tribal lands. He taught himself and his two children the more peaceful art of foraging for their food; he learned the properties of plants and honed his foraging techniques.

A true Renaissance caveman, Hoo was known amongst his clan as something of an artist: a sculptor and stonemason. He fashioned tools and sculpted statues made of stone in what spare time he had. An unnatural clearing lay outside Hoo's cave, the surrounding trees severely burnt, and here and there, groups of large rocks had become exposed. The largest rocks bore Hoo's carvings: painstakingly etched images of unusual beings and creatures, some depicted with just three fingers on their hands. His renderings were so strangely foreign that they captured the attention of his fellow tribe members, who would come to stare at Hoo's carvings and marvel while he worked.

Little goosebumps cropped up on my back and neck as I listened to the caveman speak of his life, home, and art. I had recently come across global news reports about newly discovered sites of ancient peoples. Inexplicably, these excavation sites frequently contained carved or painted depictions—pictographs, petroglyphs, geoglyphs of beings[10]. There seemed to always be a mysterious, otherworldly aura around these findings. If only scientists were more curious about past life regression! They might understand these glyphs more profoundly.

Fiona's caveman regression had been over two hours long. Yet there still seemed so much more to explore in that primitive, intuitively intelligent life. I took away a few significant elements from that second session: the caveman could communicate with animals, speaking "heart to heart," as Hoo put it; he appeared to have a healing ability with his hands, that Hoo himself did not seem fully aware of, but came to him with a natural ease akin to breathing, eating, and

---

[10] Between the years 2015-2018, approx. 400 petroglyphs or rock art carvings, dating back to roughly 10,000 B.C. or more than twelve thousand years ago, were unearthed in the hills and plateaus of India's picturesque Konkan coast. - Smithsonian magazine, October 2018; Ancient rock carvings from the eighth century and the reign of Assyrian King Sargon II, were excavated in Iraq with some rock reliefs showing a procession of gods riding both present-day and mythical animals. - National Geographic magazine, January 2020.

sleeping; and the slightly puzzling paradox that while he loved animals, Hoo intensely disliked snakes and lizards.

Sensing there was more to be gained from that life, I decided to revisit it in our next session. I planned to move Fiona along in that life through to Hoo's death experience and, from there, explore the inter-life. I had not shared my plans with Fiona, but upon arriving for her third session, the first thing she asked was if we could do a Life Between Lives Regression. I smiled inwardly, unsure which of us was reading the others' mind or communicating "heart to heart."

With the hypnotic trance well anchored, I instructed Fiona to go down a staircase, walk into the long hallway at the bottom, and then go through the same door as she did the last time. Once again, I intended for her to step into the life of the caveman called Hoo.

Hoo looked down upon the vastness of the jungle below him; the canopy of trees dappled and shimmered like sunlight reflecting off rippling water from a powerful beam of light shining above. He stood near the glittering trees while his tribe watched on from a safe distance.

I asked Hoo what he was doing. "Studying," came his distracted reply. Considering Hoo's position and that of his tribespeople farther away, I asked him if his people had chosen him to investigate this strange light or if he decided to investigate it himself.

"I decided," he said. "The light... has something to do with... me." Squinting, Hoo looked at the light, trying to determine its source. "There is something round hanging in the sky. The bottom of it shines a very strong, a very bright beam of light."

"As you watch that round thing in the sky, what else is happening?" I asked, wanting to clarify the scene better.

"It sucks me in."

"The light sucks you in? Into the round thing?"

"Yes."

"What happens then?"

There was a long pause before Hoo answered, "I don't know."

Unsure where this was leading, I pressed on, "*Allow* yourself to know. This very bright, strong beam of light has sucked you into the round thing hanging in the sky. You can't help it. There is nothing you can do. Now you are there, inside the round thing in the air. Allow *all* of your memories to surface. What comes to your awareness? Where are you?"

Hoo paused again, finding the words to match what he was experiencing, "I am sitting. On a chair. And I feel cold."

"You feel cold. Where are you? Are you inside or outside?"

"Yes. I am in a room… I—I have not seen such a room like this before…" He stopped before he finished the last word.

"Describe the room now."

"To my right, there are some machines. And a screen." Hoo's description was an unexpected union of his caveman knowledge filtered through Fiona's modern-day vocabulary.

"Look at the screen," I instructed. "Does it display anything?"

"Yes." He went silent for a time and then began to speak again hesitatingly. "It shows… a picture… of a man's head." He paused again, "There are snakes… No, wires coming out of the man's head… I think—I think it is *my* head."

"Something is stuck into your head?" It was my turn to pause. Carefully, I needed to consider what to say next. "So, you know this picture on the screen is of your head, is that right?"

"Yes."

"Can you see your head from the inside?"

"No. Just the shape of my head."

"You know something is in your head. Do you feel any sensation there, such as pain?"

"There is no pain, but I feel the same suction there as when I was sucked into this place."

"Is there anything else you see on the screen?" I asked.

"There are some lines on the picture of my head forming a grid, and in some places, there is writing on top of the picture. And there are some numbers written on another machine, a computer. It looks like measurements. But… the other computer has shapes, symbols on it. I don't understand them, and I cannot read what they mean."

It felt time to move away from the things outside Hoo's knowledge and back into his experience, so I asked, "What are you feeling sitting there?"

"Not much. They just 'work,' and I just sit here."

They? Hoo had not mentioned anyone else being with him in the room. "Are there other beings there besides you? Have you been up in this place before?"

Although Hoo had said that he hadn't seen such a room before, I know that people will often recall additional details once they become more deeply immersed in the regression experience.

"There are two others here now," Hoo replied. *Who are these other people?* I wondered. *This certainly was not the way I'd expected a caveman's life to go.* Diving into the unknown like this is one of the things that I love about my work.

Hoo paused and then answered my second question, "Four times. I have been here four times before. Sometimes I see the picture of my whole body on the screen."

"Look at those two people. Are they the same, or are they different from each other?"

"They are the same. There is one who is opening a drawer and reading from a long piece of paper. It seems to show the same information as what's shown on the screen. His face is like a triangle, pointing forward," Fiona-Hoo raised the hands to make the shape in front of her own face, "like a lizard's. And he is hairless like a lizard or a snake."

"Do they wear animal skins or clothes?"

"Yes… Something white. And they are my size or a little bit shorter."

"Can you tell if the being reading from the paper is male or female?"

"Not really. There are no explicit gender markings, but I sense both are male," Hoo answered. "The other one touching the screen using his fingers, like pressing some buttons… His hand is different than mine. It has just three fingers. Big, big fingers. With no nails."

"When he touches the screen, do things on the screen change?"

"Yes. Different colours, shapes, and symbols appear. I don't understand them."

I tried to think of other ways to gather information about what was going on. "Is your body free?" I asked.

"I can look at the screen. I can see everything, but I can't control my body."

Then I would not be able to get him to move about and explore his location. Changing tactics, I asked, "Since they have stuck something into your head, perhaps they can know your thoughts or feelings?"

I paused and watched Fiona nod her head in agreement. Seizing the opportunity to speak with the beings indirectly, I offered Hoo a suggestion, "Try right now to think some thoughts. While you sit there on that chair, think the thought, 'Who—are—you?' Then tell me when you have finished."

"Okay. I'm finished thinking it," Hoo replied.

"You will be able to receive their answer, however it occurs."

I waited. Fiona's eyes remained closed, but her eyelids fluttered as the information came through.

"The being who was reading from the paper has turned and is looking at me," Hoo shared. "His eyes are brown... And he tells me, 'Do not be scared. We just want to know things about you.'"

That did not fully answer the question, but it showed telepathic communication with these beings was possible. Moving forward with this new piece of information, I continued to draw more out of Hoo and his experience, "What is your *own* next question for them?"

"Where do you come from?"

"And you will receive their response."

"From far away," was the only answer the beings would offer. We tried again, asking for the name of a planet or a star, but their answers remained the same: they came from so far away that it was not even possible to see their constellation of origin from Earth. However, they wished to give Hoo some information that he might take back to Earth with him by encoding data into a current that would flow through the electrodes connected to Hoo's brain.

"But I still want to know where they come from." I could not be sure if it were Fiona or Hoo speaking.

"Ask them that again then."

This time Hoo received a concrete answer, and I asked Hoo to spell the name of the visitors' planet: A-L-U-C-I-F. I could not help but notice a strong similarity to the biblical name 'Lucifer," the fallen angel from Heaven. Hoo tried to pronounce the name for me, and surprisingly, it sounded like "Alantif" or "Alantis." More mythical connections! I told the caveman that many believed there was once an ancient civilization on Earth called "Atlantis."

"Yes," came Hoo's serious response. "They made it. Or we made it. They are giving us the knowledge to build Atlantis on Earth.

"Soon, they will take my clansmen, one by one, and give them the same knowledge as me so that my people will become the builders of the cities of Atlantis."

I asked Hoo if he knew these answers because of the knowledge transmitted through the electrodes. In affirming that this was the case, Hoo realized that he was also receiving wisdom and information from "another light."

"The feeling is overwhelming," Gently and softly shifting her body on my couch, Fiona said, greatly moved by Hoo's retelling of the 'Other Light.' "It's the feeling and sensation of love. Pure, unconditional love." The 'Other Light' was also easily distinguishable from the ship's searing light beam. Hoo's ability to receive information from that other 'loving' light had initially stirred the Atlantean's interest in the caveman. The triangle-faced beings wanted to know more of the knowledge and information that Hoo was receiving.

The moment Hoo discerned there were two distinct lights, and the essence of the Other Light, he no longer wanted to be examined and analyzed by the beings, and the electrodes became uncomfortable for him. I instructed Hoo to ask the beings to stop, but he simply removed the wires himself, saying, "They cannot force me. I don't like the wires, and that's what I want."

"Do they stop?" I checked in with Hoo.

"Yes," he replied.

I was keenly aware of how Hoo *now* could move freely, whereas earlier when I had questioned him, he could not. Generally, in a regression, when people believe they cannot physically move, it is only because they do not *think* they can, not because they are unable to do so. And often, to move is simply a question of deciding to do so.

I thought about Fiona's life and how much she knew and did not know about her life. I thought about how genetic information can travel down through the generations, and certain patterns can also travel across reincarnations. I continued speaking to Hoo: "There is this woman named Fiona. You may or may not know who she is, but there is a relationship between the two of you. Ask them if they implanted information or knowledge in her, as well."

"They are in the process," Hoo answered.

I instructed him to ask them to stop with her and all the reincarnations of that soul.

"They can't force what I don't want," he replied after communicating directly with the beings.

"How many other people on Earth are they doing the same process with?"

Hoo took a long time to respond, and when he eventually did, his answer was indirect: "They are sneaky. But it's very difficult for them now," he said. I began to ask a follow-up question but was immediately interrupted by him. "The machines have stopped," he stated cryptically.

"Can you connect with the Other Light, now? The one that loves unconditionally?" I wanted to move things along, but the old caveman had other ideas; he first wanted to return to this village and tell others not to agree to the brain electrodes and the implanting of information.

When he returned to Earth, Hoo lay in a chilled jungle pool; his skin had become extremely hot and needed to be 'normalized' after his encounter with the beings from the Planet Atlantis. His tribe was relieved and happy to find Hoo safely returned. Curious about what Hoo had discovered, they asked him all that he had seen, and he advised them not to allow the visitors to do anything to their bodies and minds. Some of his clan chose to listen to his wise counsel, while others did not.

I did not know whether Fiona was even aware of the term Atlantis. But I asked Hoo if *he* knew whether Atlantis would ever be built. He said that he did and that it would start being built by the generation that succeeded him.

Hoo, the caveman, lived until the age of eighty-two. On his last day, he sat down in his old, familiar spot in his cave and meditated. He never left that spot. Breathing deeply and calmly from his belly, Hoo's soul simply left his body by way of his crown chakra, just like that lifetime as a local governor.

The session had served to shed some light on many of the minor mysteries from the previous regression to the life of Hoo: We learned that the unnatural clearing in front of Hoo's cave had been formed by the star ship's powerful beam of light, baking the soil, unearthing giant rocks, and charring the surrounding trees. Hoo and his tribe had created the stone glyphs of three-fingered beings to honour the memory of a foreign visitation.

More importantly, Fiona realized several elements about herself and her life purpose: she, like Hoo, shared a dislike for lizards. She recognized the origin of that dislike came from those beings on the starship; their faces and touch had been lizard-like. Fiona had also puzzled over career choices, and although drawn to a career in the sky, she had never enjoyed flying. "It has always felt weird as if I didn't like doing it, but I had to do it." *Was that contradiction also rooted in Hoo's alien abductions?*

The divine love from the Other Light that had overwhelmed Fiona earlier continued to resonate with her afterwards. She connected that feeling to how she had felt when Wiseman Hoo had been channelling and counselling his tribespeople; "Giving voice to pure thought" was how Fiona described it.

"I always felt I should be doing something in more of a healing nature, rather than travel service work," Fiona commented as she was on her way out.

Fiona came back for two more sessions during her month of vacation. We focused on life-between-lives regression, where she went through a life review with her council of nine for both the life of Hoo and the city governor. Her council brought her to the life planning stage of the life of Fiona. She remembered more about her inner strength and learned of her aptitude for animal communication and healing.

"I don't know if I can keep being a flight attendant," Fiona told me after one of those sessions. "My colleagues are proud of the job. But I just don't care."

I reminded her, "When he no longer wanted to be there, Hoo walked away from the starship."

A year later, I received an email update from Fiona: she had started her Reiki Master training and was excited to continue exploring and developing her "healing hands." And next year, she planned on walking away from her life in the airlines, stepping more fully into her purpose as a healer.

Death Walker Julie

A Moonlight Walk

"What are you afraid of?" I asked Julie as she handed me back her intake form. She possessed a natural, elegant beauty that reminded me of the French actress Sophie Marceau. Julie was, in fact, from France, having arrived in Canada as an international student just two years before our meeting.

When she was only fifteen, Julie had lost her mother to cancer. Her father frequently travelled for work and was neither emotionally nor physically available to support his daughter through such a trying time. So, a teenage Julie with very little guidance and largely left to her own devices grew up quickly after her mother's passing.

A year later, Julie's father remarried and promptly busied himself with the joys and responsibilities of his new family. So as not to interfere with his new life, Julie was given enough money and freedom to travel and do whatever her young heart pleased. Still, all the liberty that money could afford could not buy Julie the love and affection she so sorely needed in her life.

"What am I afraid of? Many things," answered the twenty-three-year-old. "And many times, the fears do not make sense to me; I know it ties into my low self-confidence. I know I should not compare myself with others, but it seems that other people are all better than me."

"Better than you at what?" I asked.

"I—" Julie began and then paused, lost in thought. It was not her English that made Julie hesitate—she displayed an excellent command of the language—instead, Julie found it difficult to articulate her feelings.

I tried to put the young woman at ease, "I'm sure a lot of people, you included, are better than me in math. But I don't have any fear of it."

"Oh, no. I'm sure my math is not better than yours," Julie said with a laugh. "I am not at all good at math."

Good. We are alike, I thought, *all the better for establishing rapport.* "But you don't seem to be bothered by not being good at math. What are the things that matter more than math, that have you feeling not so good about yourself when others are better than you?" I prompted, learning that Julie's inner narrative was that other people were more intelligent than her. Her greatest fear was appearing stupid; it was a fear Julie struggled to manage and had come to my practice with the intention to release it once and for all.

"We don't live to be liked by others," I continued. "There's no need to judge yourself as either better or worse than anyone else."

"Yes. I know. I am trying very hard. But it seems that I have a blockage or something. I just can't manage or control my feelings," Julie said dejectedly.

"What feelings are those?"

"Fear, sadness, and anxiety."

Naming her feelings seemed to call up those emotions for Julie. Seeing it as a good moment for her to enter a trance, I had Julie comfortably recline in her chair.

"What if I can't be hypnotized?" Julie looked at me nervously as she was settling in.

"Well, almost everyone asks me that question at their first session. So—"

"No," Julie interrupted. "I actually had an experience. When I was back home. Once in a park, someone was trying to hypnotize people. It was for fun. Entertainment. He tried it on me too, but it did not work."

"What happened for it not to work with you?" I asked, looking for an answer such as "my hand couldn't get stuck to my face."

"I think I am just not hypnotizable." Instead of answering my question directly, Julie looped her thought back to a generalization.

"Well, you are here. It seems your unconscious mind disagrees that you cannot be hypnotized." I leaned towards her and lowered my voice. "If you were 'unhypnotizable,' your unconscious mind would not bring you here, for you... to *be*... *hypnotized*." I said each key phrase slowly and purposefully.

Julie looked at me a little confused, and confusion is always a hypnotist's little gateway to trance. I asked her more about what had or had not happened with the street performing hypnotist, but it was such a long time ago that Julie could not recall the details.

"Since you cannot even remember it," I continued, "Maybe you *were* hypnotized." I lightly "joked" and smiled, then instructed her to gaze at a spot on the ceiling while I suggested that her eyelids would become comfortably heavy. Her eyes now closed, I continued in my monotone and drew Julie's attention to the relaxing heaviness of her eyelids. I was preparing Julie for an eye-catalepsy challenge, a little test to see if she could relax her eyelids enough so that they would not open, even if she tried.

"No, I can't do it! I am feeling afraid!" Julie said with rising panic, her big eyes wide open again.

"You don't have to do it," I responded calmly and evenly. "We can just look at the fear." The fear was already present, and I knew this was an opportunity. I directed a wide-eyed Julie to tell me where the sensation of fear resided in her physical body. Soundlessly, Julie pointed to the area just above her heart.

"So, let's draw neutral attention to your upper chest, to that sensation there. It is not good, not bad, not right, not wrong. Let's just stay curious. Does the sensation have a colour?" I wanted to help Julie objectify the sensation.

"No. I do not see colour."

"Continue to look with curiosity at the colourless sensation in your upper chest. What do you find there? Any shape or size, if not a colour?" To lead the way, I closed my own eyes as I asked.

"It is like a… like a face, vertical."

A face? There seemed more to it.

"A vertical face… Is it the face of a male or a female?"

"A boy. But I cannot see it clearly. It is dark, like a shadow," Julie answered, her eyes closed to better focus on the face she was seeing.

"Yes, it's a shadow, but you can tell it's a boy's face. How old is the boy?" My voice stayed calm.

"I don't know…eleven or twelve… No. I could not get it clearly. This makes no sense. I am imagining it!" Again, Julie's eyes popped open.

"If you are imagining it, at least you are not consciously trying to do it. It came to you, so you may have imagined it from your subconscious mind. Therefore, it must mean something."

"But I don't know what it means. It does not work."

"To know what it means, we need to follow it all the way to find out. Not half of the way. Right now, it's too early to say. We don't need to know what it means yet, but we can go and find out. I promise you my voice will always be there with you. My voice will be your guidance." I remembered Julie had longed for guidance as a child.

That word worked like a charm. Julie finally relaxed a little and closed her eyes again.

"That's right. There is that boy's face," I said slowly and paused. "This face has a body, or a figure to it, doesn't it?"

"It is dark. And he is standing there. His face turned down toward the ground. He looks very sad and helpless."

"Maybe *you* can help him?" I suggested. Compassion was one of the things Julie had mentioned being good at during our consultation. "Can you imagine yourself going over to him and saying, 'Hello?'"

"Can I do that?" Julie asked, her curiosity taking root.

"You can try and see what happens. Remember, my voice is always with you."

"Okay."

"Does he notice you?"

"He knows I am here, but he does not care much. He is still looking sad, looking down at the ground."

"Ask him if he needs help."

"…He is indifferent."

"Since he seems to be helpless, tell him we are here to help. Now that he has help, he can't be helpless anymore."

"Who is that?" Julie's eyes opened again, staring back at me.

"Well, you are the one who is talking to him." I then thought of simply having a direct conversation with the boy through Julie, but Julie still looked far too anxious for that kind of work, yet. "You are the one talking to him. You can ask him what his name is."

This time, Julie quietly closed her eyes, a gesture to indicate she was ready to engage with the boy, "He does not answer, really. But I got... Thom? I think his name is Thom."

That was a good start: "Ask Thom where he is from."

"I am sure it is Europe... But I do not know if he was answering or if I am imagining it."

"It doesn't matter since you said you are sure. That is what matters."

"I am very confused, Kemila," Once again, Julie opened her eyes. "What is happening?"

"Well..." I quickly scanned Julie's intake form to see what she had written under the Religion field. She had written "none," and I knew how to answer her question in a way that might make more sense to her: "You found the boy in the dark place through going into the fear and sadness in your upper chest. It seems to me Thom is in your space, and he is likely already dead. Either he doesn't know it, or he doesn't know where to go. And we can help him."

"What do you mean?" Julie asked, leaning forward slightly, now more curious than afraid.

"I mean, this Thom we are dealing with may be what some would call a 'spirit.'"

"Like a ghost?" Julie asked.

"Yes. That's another word for it."

"How do we help?" Julie inquired with ever-growing curiosity.

"Close your eyes and ask Thom if he knows that he has died."

"He knows."

"Okay. Then he is simply lost. Help him look around and look above. What is there?"

I was hoping that a tunnel of light, orbs of spirit guides, winged angels or something would appear for Thom, but I knew whatever might show up, it had to first filter through Julie's receptivity.

"Only the moonlight and the stars," Julie replied. "We are walking, and I can feel the grass, see the trees."

Nice. Aligning with the tranquility of her surroundings, Julie became much more relaxed with the process. To solidify the scene for her, I asked, "Is Thom to your left or to your right as you walk?"

"To my right. But his head is still down. He does not communicate."

I was unsure what to do next, but I had promised Julie that I would guide her, so I asked, "If you stop, would he know? Would he stop as well, or would he keep walking? Try it."

"When I stop, he knows. He stops, then he continues, but much more slowly than before."

"So, he likes your company?" I questioned delicately.

"I think so. And I like walking with him too."

"So, the two of you enjoy walking like that, under the moonlight."

"Yes. The moonlight is very bright. It is a path in the forest where we are walking. The trees are dark. But I am not afraid at all!"

Because you are meant to do this, I thought. *Just as living beings can receive messages from the spirits and be helped by them, living beings can also help spirits with their transition.* It seemed that Julie was one such living being, a spirit steward. Fluidly, wordlessly,

Julie communicated with Thom, keeping him company. And all the while, I was watching her on my recliner.

Once again, Julie opened her eyes. This time she looked quite peaceful, looking into the space in front of her. Still with questions, but Julie seemed to have also found some deeper answers, and for a moment, she was silent. When Julie finally spoke, she asked what had happened to her.

"I don't really know," I answered her sincerely. "But I had the feeling that Thom came to you long ago when you were in the hospital because of your mom's cancer. Since then, you have experienced many emotions, such as fear and sadness, but they were not always yours; they might have been his. You might have experienced his emotions. That is why it felt so irrational for you, and you could not control them."

"Oh, yeah," Julie responded thoughtfully. "Every time I reacted, sad or nervous or scared, I almost always could see a figure in front of me." She stopped to process a bit more and make her own connections: "That was Thom!"

"Yes. A lot of emotions you experienced were not yours. It is time now to let them go, and let Thom go, too. There's a better place for him than hanging out with you, feeling lost and helpless, and interfering in your life. We are going to send him to a better place, and there will be someone picking Thom up from here. You have done your work today walking with Thom. Someone will come to continue the rest of the walk."

"You mean, now?"

"Yes. I mean, now." Actually, I could not think of a better time to do it. "As you continue walking with Thom in the forest under the moon and the stars, we are going to call upon—well, I'm not religious, so for the lack of better words—angels or guides or helpers of sorts, to come here and take care of Thom; to guide him to a better place, a place that he can trust and where he can find peace." I waited, holding space for Julie to direct what happened next.

"Well," Julie said after a slight pause, her eyes closed. "I am sure I am making it up. But in my imagination, I see an old man with a long, white beard like Dumbledore. But he is not Dumbledore. The old man is standing there smiling. And there are many lights. I think it is because the old man came from light. The light is all over him. Like he is spreading—no, giving out the light himself. Glowing."

That was rather good for just "imagination." I said, "There are many ways you can make this up, like a young male angel with wings. Or a female one with long hair. But you made up this old man so easily as if it came to you. That's because it was not your conscious mind that made it up; it was your unconscious mind," I paused briefly before adding, "*if* you actually made it up. So that's a good thing."

Sometimes the hardest thing for people to trust is their own natural and direct experience. We seem to trust other people's experiences, books, and media more readily than our own.

"Now, what is happening? Do you feel you can entrust Thom to this Dumbledore?" I asked.

Julie giggled, "He is not Dumbledore. He just looks like him. But yes, I can trust him." *Well, Julie, you do know.*

"What about Thom?"

"Thom is trusting him. He is walking fast towards the glowing man, and I am left behind." She stopped. "And I cannot seem to go over there."

"Of course, you can't go over there. *There* is for those who have passed on. You are still very much physically alive; you need to stay *here*. But you can wave 'Goodbye' to them."

My chest filled with warmth as I felt an almost imperceptible nod from the "Glowing Man" in my heart as if he and I were a team. Julie stayed there a bit longer, watching them go back to the light. I had her come back to the therapy room and back to her body on the recliner once they had completely gone. I guided Julie to breathe light into her upper chest and all over her body to strengthen her sense of Self. Then, I gently brought her out of hypnosis.

Julie sat up in her seat and said, mainly to herself, "It makes sense! No one told me any of this before: spirits, death, walking." She contemplated her revelation before she happily exclaimed again, "But it makes sense!"

Ironically, Julie had felt this intensely visceral and seemingly unshakeable fear in her chest, but she was perfectly calm and peaceful when the scarier ghost spirit came onto the scene. There was the feeling that something in Julie's ability or purpose was beginning to bud and emerge. *She may be a "Crossing Guide,"* I thought. *A gentle, pleasant, and compassionate twin sister to Charon of the River Styx.*

"That was what I would typically call 'Spirit Release Therapy.' Some people come to see me specifically for that kind of reason."

"It makes perfect sense now!" Julie beamed a huge smile. "Thank you so much!" She said as she stood up from the chair. "I am feeling much lighter and freer in my body now." She paused for a brief second. "I mean, it feels really good!"

"Well, I think you are feeling yourself now. If all of this was imagination, your imagination is certainly a powerful remedy for your imaginary problems." I laughed with Julie and walked her out the door and, hopefully, onto her Path.

Part 3 – Uncovering Inner Wisdom

Past Life Relationships and Friendships Brought Forth in This Life

UNCOVER verb (used with object)
- to lay bare; disclose; reveal
- to remove a cover or covering from

Mystic Tree

From My Self to Myself

Apollo's journey started with a telephone call.

Or did it?

Perhaps, his journey began much earlier in time, as we know time to be.

Apollo called my office for a telephone consultation: "…Ever since grade school, around grade six, I have been asking questions about life and who I am: Where do I come from? Why am I here? Who am I really? Why am I doing this? Why must I be born?" He told me how his last question, *"Why must I be born?"* was always accompanied by a state of emotional ambivalence. To resolve it, he thought, *"I will just play my role and be done with it."*

A social butterfly working in the arts and culture scene, Apollo felt disconnected and alone in the world. He only ever felt fleeting moments of happiness when he was with his closest friends. "I hide my feelings very well," Apollo spoke over the phone, adding that he kept his spirituality to himself, except with his closest friends.

It is more than a bit of a human paradox that we often believe we are hiding our emotions from others, yet, in truth, we are only denying and hiding our feelings from ourselves. This emotional disconnection from others and self had Apollo suffering from role confusion. A part of Apollo had benched itself from the game, watching forlornly from the sidelines.

Apollo kept receiving messages in the face of his existential crisis, seeing repetitive numbers everywhere he went. His intuition screamed at the young man, resulting in a deep yearning for hypnotherapy and Life-Between-Lives Regressions. And that was how Apollo became one the most dazzling stars in the rich sky of my practice.

I often marvel at the many layers and aspects each of us has and how we can genuinely want to deny our emotions, gifts, experiences, and responses when we repeatedly hear statements about ourselves that differ from our perception of ourselves.

Many years ago, as I was walking down Denman Street in Vancouver, a vision of a book cover came to my inner eye. The cover read, *"Layers of ...,"* with the last word or words blurred, too illegible to read. I have not yet materialized that book, but at that moment, I knew that the book, a book about how we all have to various degrees, Multiple Personality *Order*, was waiting for me to write. A book about how we sometimes hide a part of ourselves, get lost, and then seek outside, such as therapeutic help, to solve the puzzles created by our own minds.

Apollo continued his wordy narrative to me on the phone: "I took the time and read through your entire website; read through most of the many case stories on your blog pages and watched all your YouTube videos. That's when I knew that I liked your approach."

"And what is it that you are looking to get out of our work together?" I asked Apollo, a common question of mine in any client consultation.

"I just want to know what my lessons are to learn in this lifetime," he said, responding with one of the most popular answers. "Like, what is my purpose and higher fulfillment? I want—I need to find it out."

Apollo desperately needed to restore a deeper connection with himself and, from there, regain his balance so that he could move forward in a more authentic and integrated way. The young man had been doing what he could towards achieving that goal through reading books by Michael Newton and others. The role I could play in Apollo's soul searching was to create a safe, healing environment where he could experience having a deeper, more open, emotional connection with himself and tap into his inner wisdom, finding his own answers.

When he arrived for his session, I met a tall, handsome, charming young man. Apollo had never done a hypnotherapy session before, and our phone conversation had left me uncertain about where exactly to start the process. "I know you are very invested in life-between-lives, and that's probably where you'd like to find answers to all the questions you have," I began my explanation of my preferred approach with Apollo. "That is a pure spiritual state, and sometimes it's hard to put into words what you perceive. Words, after all, are the product of this time-space-physical-reality.

"When you get beyond what is physical, it is not easy to use human words to explain the non-physical, especially when you have not had this type of experience before. So, one stepping-stone down the subconscious memory lane is through a Past Life Regression. It's still a spiritual regression, but you will perceive yourself having a physical body, living a physical life, which makes it much easier to make sense of and verbalize."

"Sure," Apollo responded with ready agreement. "Anything you think will be helpful!"

I knew the artistic, poetic Apollo might find the regression process relatively easy and might discount his subconscious mind.

"It may feel like you are making everything up as we go along," I began to clarify. "But there will be a smooth quality to it, not like when you think hard to make something up. There will be a flow to what's coming up, and many times, the scene unfolding will have an emotional component to it." Apollo nodded his head in understanding.

"So, here's the couch," I proceeded with my standard instruction, "This is your couch now, and you can do whatever you like to it to make yourself comfortable. Some people choose to sit up; some choose to lie down. Whatever you do, make sure it will make you comfortable." Apollo lay down on the couch, pulled the blanket over his body, and started to giggle.

"This is real now. Wow! It's like a movie. Like I'm in a movie, on a therapist's couch…" He giggled some more.

"Yes. Like a movie." I then shifted into my hypnotic voice. "And this movie starts here and continues somewhere else. And ends in yet another surprising place…"

As my speech slowed, I matched Apollo's breathing. Relaxed by my voice, his eyes automatically closed, and his body comfortably rested on the couch. I instructed his unconscious mind to take us to a favourite place:

"It's in nature… There are willow trees… I am by a slow river… It's very calm… There are mountains in the distance…" Apollo described his favourite place slowly, taking long pauses between each statement. His tone indicated he was already deep in a trance.

"The further you walk, the deeper you go… down the River of Time," I said, my voice in pace with his, taking the liberty of naming the river while I was at it. "Over there, across the River of Time, is a bridge, way down there. And eventually, when you come to the bridge, you will cross it. And across the bridge, over the River of Time, you will find yourself in another time, at another place, living in another body, in another life." I gave Apollo's subconscious mind a direction, "It will be the most significant lifetime in terms of your purpose and higher fulfillment." That was all that was needed for Apollo to drift gently into another lifetime.

Kamal walked through a vast desert, alone except for his camel, under the cover of dazzling stars. He was young, twenty-five years old, and wearing an alabaster thawb and turban. He did not know where his feet were guiding him, and it did not seem to matter either. Finally stopping, Kamal lay to rest on a nearby dune, his camel spitting and kneeling beside him. Stretching out his bronze arms, he nestled his head in the cradle that they made. Looking up to the night sky, gazing at the stars and the enormity of the universe, Kamal felt a sense of awe and the sublime; a sense of connectedness to the cosmos. Kamal was at peace under the lush carpet of stars, quickly drifting off to sleep with a beatific smile. The night sky filled him in his sleep, the vastness of the desert seated inside him.

Kamal woke the next day, happy and content. His travels finally took him to a bustling desert marketplace. Kamal roamed through the mess of shoppers, merchants, and stalls. He eventually stopped long enough to buy some bread, sit down on a low wall to eat, and wash the meal down with a long, slow swig of water before resuming his wanderings. The sun was approaching its zenith, and Kamal decided to duck inside a teahouse for some refreshments and rest during the heat of the day. He spoke with no one, ordering his tea in silence. Finding an available seat on one of the low, lavishly tapestried sofas, Kamal pulled out his battered, leather-bound journal and a pair of wire-rimmed spectacles. Already one-third of his way into the old, brown journal, Kamal diligently documented his travels. "Little scribblings here and there, nothing too significant," Kamal explained. "Just my thoughts. I write about my thoughts. I take the words of my thoughts and transpose them into verse, into poetry."

"What do you follow when you travel, Kamal?" I asked the wanderer. "A map? The wind? Your inner compass?"

"I do not follow; I simply go where the journey takes me. And by some unknown means, I just know where to go."

"Maybe you follow the stars," I humorously postulated, as Kamal joined me in a warm, full-bodied laugh. "When the sun goes down a little, and it becomes cooler, you finish your tea, and you leave this tea house. Where do you go next?" I continued to probe.

"I turn left and keep going; I keep walking."

"In which direction? The desert again? Or somewhere else?"

"I see a city. It is coming into view on the horizon. The city is all white and entirely beautiful. Its milky white walls and architecture twinkle like quartz in the sun. And there is a mighty palace.

"The city is truly noisy, but I walk my camel through it. People poke their heads out of windows and doors, as I do, and small children stare down at me from above." I wondered if Kamal was describing an actual city in North Africa or somewhere in the Middle East. "I look up to see merchants selling shoes," he said, giving me a wanderer's take on the walled city.

Kamal wandered the serpentine streets and alleys until he came upon a large, arched entryway. He craned his neck, looking up as he passed under the arch's lintel, gauging how high it might be. Laid out before him was a dizzying mosaic of tiny, white houses crowding the terrain. It was like a madman's maze with walls going off at all angles, creating a disorienting optical illusion of overlapping lines. Thoughtfully, Kamal considered a course through the vertiginous maze and then let his feet guide him to where he might want to go. Struck by the sweeping presence of a resplendent, crescent-roofed building, Kamal emerged from the labyrinth at long last. It was a grand palace, and all Kamal could do was stand and stare.

"What does it evoke in you when you look at it?" I asked the young traveller.

"It is divine!" He replied, awestruck. "It imbues a sense of vastness, of the eternal and infinite. The stars and deserts, the palace, the city, they are all sublime. I am drawn to it."

I noted that Kamal had still not interacted with anyone in the city, and I wanted to know why. "I am not so much drawn to their faces. Mostly, it is architecture and nature that calls to me." Kamal remained standing and staring in front of the wrought iron and spiked palace gates. I could not tell whether he had finally arrived at his destination.

"If anyone from the city asks you where you come from, what would you tell them?" I asked, knowing he was not keen to interact with the city's occupants.

"I come from the land of the lands," came his enigmatic reply. There was a pause, and then Apollo came through, laughing, "I don't know what it means. I just said what came to my mind."

Ignoring Apollo, I directed my next question at Kamal, "If they ask, 'Is the land of the lands far?' What do you say?"

"'You will know it when you know it,' I smile. I do not explain." It sounded so Zen-like, as Kamal was simply relaying without filters. I knew that Apollo would be a fitting energy conduit.

"Do they understand when you answer them like that?"

"They look at me strangely; one old man scratches his head and walks away."

I got straight to the point, "Kamal, where are you going?"

"Journey to the East perhaps, I might find something there, but I do not know what," Kamal said, giving me one of his now famously vague answers.

But I am nothing if not persistent and patient when I need to be. "Are you halfway there yet?"

"No. I just started." A true journey indeed! I decided to move Kamal forward in time to see if he had reached his desired destination.

The East was entirely different and new, swaddled in a deep and boundless forest. A multitude of streams networked through the soaring vastness of trees. And though the sun shone brightly up above, only a few bold rays streaked the leaves and dappled the dark forest floor. Kamal walked peacefully amongst the trees, breathing deeply in the pure, clean air. Eventually stopping to settle on a flat, mossy rock, Kamal sat, eyes closed, palms up, and meditated for a long while. He sat so still and for so long that a small, blue bird touched down to rest on his shoulder. It was the bird, however, who began to get restless first. Preening, then fluttering its wings, and finally taking flight to hover just a stone's throw away from Kamal's head. Kamal opened his eyes and rose in one fluid motion.

"I will follow the bird," he informed me. "I trust the bird. For the bird will show me the way." And the bird flew as Kamal faithfully followed. The bird led Kamal, stopping now and again to land on a branch, waiting for Kamal to catch up. He looked up and began to converse with it: "You have to hold the way up," he said to the little bluebird.

When a person's mind is at ease with things that do not make sense, I know they are in a state of deep trance; no longer burdened by their everyday overthinking analytical mind.

The bird waited, sentient of what the young man was asking. The two walked and flew on through the deep forest, the bluebird trilling a sweet song as the wind rustling the leaves of the trees offered up its chorus. Kamal's heart felt so light that he thought he might fly away like the bird. He felt a connection to the great trees overhead. He could sense them whispering the same message to one another, vacillating from tree to tree until it reverberated throughout the entire forest. Until Kamal finally understood its meaning: *"Go inside, go inside the tree."* And he obliged.

I became doubtful whether I should continue to treat Apollo's journey like a past life regression. The entire session had not been a typical regression: Kamal was alone and adrift, disconnected from any other human he encountered. There was little drama, no human interaction, and now he had walked *into* a tree! Sensing some spiritual experience to come, I knew there would be no need to bring the life of Kamal to its death sequence that would escort us to his life-between-lives experience. In that tree in the middle of the forest, all Apollo's questions might be answered.

"So, you become a tree," I echoed to Kamal.

"Yeah, just," he paused as if distracted. The winds died down, and the little bird ceased its trilling, gliding down to land on a majestic tree in the heart of the deep forest. It sat and waited for Kamal. The young man never hesitated, never broke his easy stride. He just walked, stepping into the massive tree. "I feel there is learning for me here," Kamal reasoned. "I am in the tree simply because I desired to learn the connections of life. I can feel its branches and the expansiveness of its roots underneath the cool, aliveness of the soil.

"The fungi, all of the life forms beneath the earth, just like the tree, are teaching me," Kamal paused to breathe in the many interconnected sensations of his surroundings. "This is what it feels like when we are connected," he whispered. "It feels electric, the harmony of the vibrations of nature… My soul is so very, very stirred…" Kamal broke off sobbing, a powerful surge of indescribable emotion overtaking him.

"The tree… is showing me… I am *feeling*… all the connections…" Kamal continued in his broken way, "I can see… it now makes sense… *Just feel*… peace… joy… absolute love…" Kamal's inner awareness had exploded wide open. He could feel and know the great synchronicity of the natural world, of how perfectly everything worked, the web-like roots of the tree branching ever outward, a web of connectivity. The creatures on earth and still waters below, air and sky above its branches and leaves, were all interconnected with the tree and Kamal. He felt all those connections accompanied by feeling nothing but pure, unconditional love. Love of passion and happiness, of peace and appreciation, love abounded. And Kamal wept great tears, consumed with love, engaged in harmonious oneness.

I sat quietly, feeling blessed and grateful for Kamal for having this experience. I waited silently, allowing the experience to solidify within Kamal-Apollo's psyche so that he would always remember how it feels to be connected, moving forward in the life of Apollo, despite how alone he may have felt before.

"So, this is it—What you came here to learn?" I asked, finally breaking the silence. "Allow this experience to guide your inner knowing for higher fulfillment. The connectedness is such that even the different versions of lives are interconnected within your soul. So, you can allow this experience to guide your life as Apollo with higher purpose and fulfillment. Kamal's is the life with significance: simple, straightforward, easy, no distraction, yet profound all the same. Walking into a tree, yet you are not a tree in appearance. In this intimate connectedness, any question is answered. When I ask a question, allow the answer to flow through you, now."

"I am there folding my arms, holding my heart. And my heart senses the tree," Kamal responded blissfully.

"Let the tree tell you something about yourself."

"It tells me: 'Everything is good. Just like the smallest of my roots, you cannot see them, but they are still there. And *you* are a part of all this. You will not be lost. You will not be lost, my child. Trust now and know. You are part of one with everything. Even though you are on the other side of the bank, yet the river flows.'" Apollo wept again.

"What type of tree is this?" I asked.

"It's an oak tree. It's very, very old, and it tells me, *'My child, you will know.'*"

"So, ask the tree, 'Why am I here?'" The question Apollo had asked since he was in elementary school.

"It doesn't tell me. It just shows me a spiral, pointing outward, like a snail's shell, only a lot denser. 'It's all connected,' the tree says. 'None of you are separate. Even though you may be far out on the spiral, you are still a part of the spiral.'"

"Another question for the tree is, 'Where do I come from?'"

"'We come from the lands,'" responded the tree.

I moved on to another question an eleven-year-old Apollo had asked: "Who am I really?"

"'You are a soul,'" said the tree and Apollo added, "And that I know!"

"Why do I feel this is not home?"

"'Because you forgot it!'"

"Why must I be born?" I asked from my notes the last question of Apollo's.

"'Because they need you. You know how hard it is, but...'" His voice becoming inaudible, tears interrupted the tree's channel and streaked down Apollo's handsome face. I knew Apollo was accessing and integrating the tree's answers on his own. The answers differed from what Apollo had previously said: "Theoretically, I know I chose this life." The responses were more authentic, natural, and evocative than any spiritual platitude.

Apollo sat up, wiping his face with some tissues, as I brought him out of hypnosis. "I know what you mean now when you said it would feel like I'm making it up. Did I make it all up?" He asked, looking up at me. I knew Apollo's experience had been both real and profound, yet his human self needed validation that an experience so powerful and expansive could indeed be real.

Generally, I do not feel I am in a position to provide an answer to such a question because, one way or another, the person could choose to believe I am rationalizing "the irrational." So, I simply remarked, "If you did, your subconscious mind must be an incredible storyteller."

Our session ended. Apollo got up to head out but remembered something just before he got to the door. He pulled his phone out of his pocket and showed me his social media profile photo: Apollo hugging a huge tree. "I just changed my profile photo a short time ago. Isn't that synchronicity?" He laughed, shaking his head lightly, and left my office with a broad smile on his face.

Later the next day, Apollo sent me a text message:

> Kemila, there was something kinda weird and interesting (in a synchronistic kind of way) on my way to work this morning. Is it strange that I think I may have seen "Kamal" (Or someone who looks like the picture of Kamal whom I described last night)?

> This morning, when I was taking the exact same route I take every single day, just when I was waiting for some crowds to pass, I initially saw a man (Middle Eastern/Indian) dressed in a mid-length robe that fell below the waist. It was in the brightest, neon orange colour. The brightness of that neon orange robe caught my attention because of its colour and the uniqueness of the clothing style. He stands out in a crowd where everyone else was wearing "everyday" attire.

> The man stops, turns his head back, and looks like he is waiting for someone or something. Then my gaze looks up, and sees an Arabian/Middle Eastern young man, in his mid-late 20s, wearing the same kind of robe as the first man, but this time in an off-white, cream colour.

> And, I instantly thought, "That's him…" Then the scene
> was over, and the two men just walked on and by.

Perhaps, Apollo needed to be shown that it was real, not a story birthed by his imagination. Or maybe, "reality" was beginning to thin for Apollo, and other realities were now more easily bleeding through. I knew that Apollo was up for whatever was coming his way, and I was thrilled that we had met. As if reading my thoughts, a moment later, Apollo sent me a follow-up text message:

> Last night on my way home from our session, I felt this incredible sense of serenity, joy, and heightened awareness. Then for some reason, a BMO, "Bank of Montreal" sign caught my attention. The last four letters of "MontREAL" seemingly appeared clearer and brighter compared to the rest of the words. Then shortly after that, I passed by "Shi ZHEN ya"[11] (a sushi restaurant) and felt like the sign spoke to me as well. It's as if my subconscious was answering my own conscious mind's question of "Was that real?" (I almost couldn't believe the magic that transpired over the two hours). Then I realized, on this stage of Life, it is what one chooses to make "real."

I could not have said it better than that! Later, I told Apollo how his experience of going into the tree reminded me of the sci-fi concept of "grok"[12] or "grokking." Apollo messaged me back:

---

[11] *Zhen* in Mandarin translates to the word, "real".

[12] Author, Robert Heinlein coined the so-called Martian word, "grok" in his 1961 science fiction novel, *Stranger in a Strange Land*, and it is said to mean, "to understand something so profoundly through intuition alone; to empathize with another from such a deep degree, that you merge with them."

Kemila, an epiphany came to mind just now (even though it has been right under our noses all this time, like the answer has been there all along, clear as day but I just couldn't see it before).

We, humans, by coming into being, are all "grokking" so to speak. Our spirit enters the physical flesh to learn, experience, and come to know this form and the wisdom that emerges from this experience. That's why there's amnesia, so the experience could be fully experienced in its truest sense; otherwise, it would be hard, if not impossible to convince ourselves, our souls. It's really an act of benevolence, and above all, trust, and ultimate patience. Trust in each soul, that no matter what, ultimately, we will all "remember" where we've come from after we have learned from this human form, in this school.

Sanaa's Book of Life

Healing: Resistance to Release

Intentionally or spontaneously, going into an after-death scene can easily occur during a past life regression. A person may go directly to an immediate after-death moment at the beginning of a regression. Sometimes, this happens when I instruct them to "move forward in time to the next significant event in that lifetime." Instead, they move forward to a moment after physical death, arguably a "significant event." In some cases, they do not even know that they are dead! Perhaps, the M. Night Shyamalan film, *The Sixth Sense* was not simply pure fiction.

There is always confusion for the client and sometimes for the hypnotherapist when this happens. But if the hypnotic state is deep enough, the client can describe what comes to their awareness without conscious interference.

One such example was Sanaa, a high school teacher who came to my office seeking help with her social anxiety. She frequently suffered from panic attacks, especially when thrust into unanticipated situations, like travelling, being alone and doing anything new. Sanaa's anxiety had always been with her. More recently, it had intensified because she was trying to conceive.

A practicing Muslim, Sanaa was not sure what to make of "past lives." Reincarnation or transmigration is a grave disbelief or kufr in Allah. Before she booked her first appointment with me, though, she had browsed through my website and knew that I helped people visit their past lives. Despite it being all over my website, I do not usually initiate discussing past lives with my clients, and it was not until our fourth session that Sanaa broached the subject herself. When she did mention it, she alluded to past lives in almost a negative way: "…But past life stuff can't be true." That brief remark was all the alert that I needed. Whenever a person initiates a subject, they often have a subconscious curiosity. Or even a fascination with it, regardless of how their conscious mind perceives and judges the matter.

Sanaa admitted that she was fascinated by past lives but was uneasy and uncertain whether she should allow herself to believe in reincarnation or not.

"Or, more clearly," she added with a nervous giggle, "Maybe I just don't have a past life. Maybe this is my first life ever." Sanaa's clarification reminded me of people who say they do not believe in God but still fear God's wrath.

"Well, the best way to know the unknown is to find out," I said to the lady with anxiety issues. "And hypnosis is a very good tool with which to explore this. If you are open, we can explore it together; it may even prove relevant to your presenting issues," I said, knowing that we had yet to sufficiently uncover the root cause of Sanaa's anxiety and panic attacks during our three previous sessions.

Hesitant to commit to an answer, Sanaa did not jump in with a "Yes." Still, she did not say "No," either. I felt a happy compromise might be to take Sanaa to her "Inner Sanctuary," and we could flow anywhere from there; showing Sanaa the way to her inner sanctuary would take the stress off having to "perform."

Having someone go to their Inner Sanctuary is a method I have developed and often use in my practice. It can be any place in a client's inner or outer worlds: a real place the person has been to, a real place the person wishes to go to, or an entirely imagined place. I do not define what an inner sanctuary looks like for my clients. Instead, I encourage their subconscious minds to present a place that feels good and safe. This helps a person access their inner resources and wisdom during a session. It can also become a tool in their wellness toolbox, providing ongoing support in their life. One way of looking at the value of accessing one's inner sanctuary is that it opens another inner dimension for the person so that they may trust themselves and their subconscious more moving forward.

Sanaa's subconscious mind took us to a den or library-like room; the image of her Inner Sanctuary came through to her with crystal clarity: "It's a cool looking room. There is a short set of stairs, two or three steps, leading down to some leather sofas. The ambient lighting is slightly dim, and there are bookshelves everywhere! Wall-to-wall bookshelves."

A *very appropriate place for a teacher,* I thought as Sanaa described her sanctuary: "There is a big red, fuzzy blanket right in front of me, where there is a cozy reading spot.

"There's this beautiful, rich, beige and red carpet, too, like one of those really classic Persian ones. It's like a scene from the eighties, but it makes me feel happy, warm, and cozy. Oh, and there's this fireplace further over. There's no window, no kitchen, just a room. But I can live here."

What a wonderfully rich inner sanctuary! "Go through the books on the shelves," I instructed Sanaa. "Are they categorized? Or are they random?"

"There are a lot of topics. Everything is in fine order and visually pleasing. They look orderly, clean, and nice."

"Are you familiar with all these books?"

"Yeah. There are classic tales by Jane Austin and Shakespeare, biographies, true crime... even a teen section."

"Okay. Right now, I'd like you to find the most comfortable seat." It was time for Sanaa to relax more into the process.

"I'm lying down already," she giggled contentedly.

"Okay. You are lying there in this cozy, comfortable space. The fireplace is happily crackling. The room feels very warm and secure, and you are surrounded by all the shelves of books. You didn't know you were going to come to this room before you came here, did you?"

"Oh no."

"And yet this room has been waiting for you all this time, even when you weren't aware that it existed. That's how you can always trust your inner mind, your unconscious mind." I let that thought linger before resuming: "Now, lying there comfortably in your space, you can continue on with that trust. When you get even more relaxed, in a moment, there is one bookshelf you will find *over there.*"

I did not know where "over there" meant literally, but my clients always seem to understand and know precisely what that suggestion means to them. It instills them with more confidence in me as their guide by creating the sense that I am there experiencing things with them.

"On *that* bookshelf, there's this book about you, not you as Sanaa, but you, the deeper, expansive soul-being.

"Maybe it's another shelf. They all look similar, to begin with, but when you really look, in a moment, when you go there, you will find the right book." I paused for a moment, being mindful to keep the pacing of my instruction in alignment with Sanaa's movements. "That's right," I started again. "*That* book will be about your soul's journey. You might be surprised when you find that book. It is not going to be ordinary. When you find and open that book, you may find that you are opening a sort of magical book. You may see words, pictures, or even 3-D motion pictures. Furthermore, you may even hear sounds and smell scents."

I presented enough possibilities for Sanaa's subconscious mind to gain a greater sense of the book, no matter how her mind best formulated the information it was receiving.

"You'll be opening the book to a page: it will show you in another place, at another time; another you in another body. Let me know when you are ready." It was a subtler way to see whether Sanaa could step into a past life.

"Okay. I am ready," Sanaa said a little nervously, so I suggested that she would know the book at the right time, and not a moment earlier or a moment later. She would just *know* it when she knew it, and my voice would be there with her the whole time.

"Trust your inner knowing," I continued with anchoring the suggestion. "The book is waiting for you. Let me know when you find the book.

"I have no idea if the book is thick or thin. But you'll intuitively find the book, and when you do, take it to the coffee table and open it. You will intuitively open it to the right page. You'll know when you know.

"The page will show you something that will represent some key to this life and the anxiety in this life of Sanaa. Trust the process and your own inner mind."

"I found the bookshelf. There aren't many books on it. And the books are all different from those on the rest of the bookshelves."

"Is there one book that speaks to you? That you feel drawn to?" I probed.

"Uh-huh."

"It's a book that will have some significance to you as Sanaa."

"I feel strongly inclined to choose this 12×12 graphic book."

"Yes, that's it. You can take that book to the coffee table, where you'll flip through it, and the right page will open itself up to you."

"Okay," Sanaa went through the move from the bookshelf to the coffee table. "The book is weighty, like about five pounds."

I asked Sanaa to take a deep breath and, when ready, intuitively open the book to the right page. Sanaa burst out with a hint of relief, "The pages are all blank! Like all of them. Blank!" I was about to agree with Sanaa that this life might indeed be her first lifetime on Earth, but then she continued, "You know those really old books, with the yellowy pages? The pages of my book are like that. But they are blank! No lines, nothing."

I considered that Sanaa's general anxiety and anxiety about past life regression might have created the book's blank pages. I could accept that the pages were blank. Still, the yellowing oldness of the pages indicated something else, and I took a step back to reorient my questioning: "So maybe this book is not a book, but an unused old notebook, waiting for you to write and tell your stories?"

"This book itself must have existed for a long time," Sanaa said, exploring the dimensions of the book. "I have this feeling... it's very weird... like this book is from the nineteen-twenties. Like that is the era that it came from, but there's nothing in it. It doesn't give me any explicit indication about time or place."

That was the signal I needed from Sanaa; being a Past Life Regressionist sometimes feels like a detective or investigator. Sanaa thought there was nothing to those "blank" pages of the book but still sensed that the book was from the nineteen-twenties.

"If there is nothing there, then how did you get the 1920s?"

"When I place my hand on the page, I feel like it is from the 1920s. Or the early 1900's? It's just so weird."

"Very good. Close the page now," I instructed, changing course again. "What's on the cover?"

"It's maroon. It's got a kind of velvety feel to it. But there's nothing on the cover. It's just a plain maroon cover. I don't know why that book spoke to me in the first place!"

"An almost 100-year-old, empty book—maybe the book was encoded with some information so that nobody else would be able to open and read it but you?

"With your energy infusing the book, you will be able to decode it, and in a moment, at the right time, the book will unfold itself."

"What do you mean?"

I realized I was speaking some sort of coded language myself. There was only one thing left for me to try—placing Sanaa's hand back onto the page.

"What I mean is that you open the book again, back to that page, and place your hand on the page. After the book recognizes your energy, something will materialize on the page. Maybe you have lived in the twenties?"

"I think so."

Now we were getting somewhere. "As you continue to place your hand on the page, the page will eventually show you something. It may be vague at first, but eventually, out of all that blankness, a shape or a picture will start to take place. Whatever that is, you will know if it's daytime or nighttime."

"Middle of the day, it seems."

"That's right, middle of the day. Is this inside or outside?"

"Outside." Sanaa's hand moved along the invisible planes of the page, pointing. "I'm in a town. It's the United States. There's a building. I see stairs going down."

"Follow the stairs," I instructed, getting Sanaa to 'jump' into the page.

Sanaa was Sophia, a 19-year-old in 1921, dressed in tightly laced, shin-high, brown leather boots, a frock that went all the way down to her ankles, and a fashionable, bonnet-style hat. She felt the dress was too formal and restricting. Ridiculous, really, on such a sweltering day.

I understood how something formal could be restricting for this soul. Sanaa's long, dark hair was dyed a flamboyant, calypso blue.

Jocelyn, a wealthy young woman of the same age, often styled her attendant in the latest fashions of high society whenever the two ladies went into town. "Oh well," Sophia sighed. "Jocelyn is a very nice person. A lovely person. She treats me more like a sister or a companion than a servant. I am very, very fortunate, blessed to have been hired by her and her family.

"She always desires to protect me. That is why she dressed me this way because she did not wish for others to look down on me when we go out. But it does not feel natural for me." Sophia concluded, a little misty-eyed, her emotions welling up over the deep gratitude she felt towards Jocelyn.

"What's more natural for you then?"

"A plainer, more comfortable dress like I wear at home. This is so fancy and uncomfortable. I feel like a charlatan. And I am getting attention that I am not used to."

"After this shopping is done, where do you go?"

"We have to hurry home. Jocelyn's mother is expecting us for something. I think it's a—" She hesitated, "—a dress fitter for Jocelyn. There is going to be a dinner party."

Sophia stood duteously close to the tea salon's door as Jocelyn's parents received a would-be suitor for their daughter. It was a quiet, intimate reception with just the parents, Jocelyn, and their respective attendants. Jocelyn's parents were hopeful. Now nineteen, the fair Jocelyn was swiftly becoming too old to be eligible for marriage, and the young man present was of good breeding and might make their daughter a suitable husband. Yet, standing quietly against the wall, Sophia instinctively felt an intuition about the young man.

"There's something 'off,' creepy about him."

"But Jocelyn likes him?"

"Yes. This Mr. Belanger knows the right things to say in front of her. He smiles the right way. And he laughs at her jokes, even though they are not funny. It feels practiced and disingenuous.

"And Jocelyn is such a girly girl. She likes the attention and is accustomed to a fancy lifestyle. She's just taking it all in, lapping up the attention. Mr. Belanger behaves like a proper gentleman, but something is definitely not quite right about him."

I moved Sophia forward in time to see if Jocelyn and the not-quite-right-Mister-Belanger got married. A little surprisingly, they had not. "What happened?" I asked Sophia.

"I do not know! But Jocelyn is very sad. And it must be the same year because she is still nineteen."

"I'm sure she doesn't mind sharing with you why she is sad," I nudged, prying for a little more information.

"The strange thing is, she does not seem to see me. She is sitting there, crying, calling for me, 'Sophia, Sophia, Sophia.' I am standing right there, but she does not respond to me. Did I do something wrong?! Maybe she is angry at me?" Sophia asked in a strangled, panicky voice. "Is it my fault that she is still unwed?"

That was an indication that Sophia had died, not being seen, or heard by the living, but she had not realized or remembered it yet. Past Life Regression is not only helpful for the current life to learn from the past, but it can also serve as a release for past life personality hangovers and trapped energy. In Sophia's case, her panic attacks presenting as a symptom in Sanaa's current life.

Needing more information for context, I moved Sophia back to the event responsible for the marriage proposal falling through: "Oh dear!" Sophia gasped, "This is… Oh! He is in the kitchen. Mister Belanger is in the kitchen with me, and he is trying… Oh no! I try… to push him away. He has a kitchen knife, a big one! He is threatening me. He tells me that I have to listen to him. That Jocelyn values my opinion, and I cannot tell her anything bad about him."

"What do you know about him that is bad?"

"He stole money."

"He stole money from Jocelyn?"

"Yes."

"How do you know it?"

"I saw him do it. He took the money out of the family safe. I was carrying Jocelyn's laundry up to her room. I don't know where Jocelyn was, and I do not even know why Mr. Belanger was in the manor.

"There is a safe Jocelyn's father has in his study. And Mr. Belanger was taking out the money. He turned around and saw me standing there in the doorway, looking at him. It makes sense now... Mr. Belanger is not what he pretends to be. He is not right for Jocelyn."

Sophia dropped her basket of laundry and ran away then, with the Mr. Belanger chasing the startled maid through the manor's hallways, servant quarters, and finally into the kitchens. Something palpable shifted in Mr. Belanger's demeanour when he ground to an abrupt halt in the main kitchen. His gait slowed to a menacing swagger as Belanger gingerly picked up a cleaver off the cook's cutting board. He tapped the large knife in measured intervals along the broad, wooden tabletop, uttering a cloying, word-less summons to Sophia. He advanced on the maid in that predatory manner until she ran out of floor space in front of the sink on the kitchen's far wall. Sophia stood trembling and shaking with terror, the cold, cracked edge of the porcelain sink digging deeper into her spine. When

Belanger was only a hair's width away from Sophia's face; he sniffed the girl's hair, laughed a callous laugh, and leaned in to press the knife into the side of her neck.

"I am. So. Terrified," Sophia gasped out the words. "He is. So... Much bigger. And taller. Than me. I have never. Been. So. Afraid. In all my life!" There was no need for Sophia-Sanaa to relive her trauma in every excruciating detail, so referring to her in the third person, I gave my instruction instead: "We will drift away from the book for now. Remember you jumped into the book? Let's jump out of the book now. So, you can know, in the book, did Mr. Belanger kill Sophia or not?"

"Yes," Sanaa replied, her breathing less belaboured than moments before. "Yes, Belanger attacked Sophia first. He threw her across the room, turned her around and pushed her face down against the big kitchen table, where he raped her at knifepoint. And when he was done having his way with her, he killed her with that same knife."

"Now you know why Jocelyn couldn't see Sophia when she was right in front of her?"

"Yeah," Sanaa sighed.

After his grievous crimes, Mr. Belanger escaped the manor and was never seen again. The household believing the murdered maid to be the unwitting witness to a robbery, surmised Sophia was simply at the wrong place, at the wrong time. And Jocelyn never knew why her dashing and eligible marriage candidate had suddenly disappeared without a word.

I momentarily floated Sanaa back into the page to say a final goodbye to the body and her friend, Jocelyn. She was surprised to learn that Jocelyn was not angry with Sophia and did not blame her maid but was crying more at the loss of her friend and maid, Sophia, than for her missing fiancé. I asked Sophia if she wanted to move on, and she replied that she did, but first, she had some parting words for Jocelyn:

"I just want to thank you for always being so nice to me. For being so generous and kind; for treating and protecting me like a sister would. For wanting to make sure that people did not judge me or be unkind to me because of my status. I want to thank you, from the bottom of my heart, for always standing up for me. You are so wonderful and far beyond what I would have expected. I want you to know that you will be happy, that you will find love again, and you and I will meet again, someday." With those final words, I had Sanaa look deeply into Jocelyn's eyes. Sanaa instantly recognized the soul and identified Jocelyn from her past life as her good friend Michelle in her current life.

Now, the soul was ready to move on to where it belonged. There were two guides there to assist with the journey; one called Brianne and the other, David. Both were present to help the soul with her life review. The simple lesson of that life of Sophia was that it was okay to be innocent and pure, that she need not be someone she was not. Happiness was, and is, in the being of who you want to be.

The guides showed brief flashbacks of Sophia's life: those little moments when Sophia was simply being herself, heedless of her social status or earthly gains. I brought the session to a close after Sophia's life review, but I could easily see how the message was also applicable to Sanaa's life. Now that the guides had revealed themselves, I sensed that there was more we could explore in the life of Sophia, too. So, when Sanaa came back to my office for her fifth session, I suggested that we might pick up where we left off in our previous session and that, with the help of her guides, we go further into Sophia's earlier life.

This time it was much easier for Sanaa to trust herself and enter that past life. We started by inviting in her two guides, David and Brianne. The guides pointed to a screen, which displayed images of how Sophia had lost her parents at an early age; how Jocelyn's mother had taken the poor orphan into her household, caring for and rearing her. First as a playmate for Jocelyn, and later, as she grew older, as her maid. The girls were happy together, but Sophia carried a deep sadness with her at no longer having her parents around to guide her and watch her grow.

I asked Brianne and David how Sophia's life review might also be related to Sanaa's anxiety. "The fear of not feeling safe," they answered in unison, "When she didn't know or understand what was going to happen to her after her parents died."

"How might Sanaa go about living her life now, knowing it is now safe?" I asked the guides further.

"What is done is done," Brianne answered alone this time. "You need to let go, Sanaa," she continued, taking Sanaa's hands into her own. "The life of Sophia and the life of Sanaa were and *are* two different lives.

"What happened, happened. You cannot control it. To try and control it will only cause you pain. But you can control how you feel in your present now.

"Life is full of the unexpected, of risk and the unknown. That is the adventure you came here to experience. You cannot stop living because of fear. It will only take you out of the many possible joys and wonder and excitement of your present."

Sanaa did not seem to buy into the wise words of her guides. Their words were coming through her, but her energy did not match them. "You were not convinced, were you?" I said to Sanaa, seated in front of me.

"No," she laughed hollowly. "It's easy for someone to say that. But unless you actually feel the panic, you don't know it. I understand all of what they say. I can even say and mean those things to other people. But to live it when it happens is an entirely different thing."

Change is a process, a process some people genuinely enjoy, rather than the alternative of rushing headlong towards the result. Sanaa had visited two other hypnotherapists before seeing me for the same issues. She told me how she liked them and had received good results with them. Still, she was trying yet another one. I started to suspect that Sanaa was one of those people who enjoy the process of change, even though she just did not know it consciously.

I had written down a note to myself on Sanaa's first visit: 'Sanaa craves and loves attention. Maybe she is using hypnotherapy to provide that?' Her anxiety attacks and the seriousness in which she had described her issues aside, Sanaa, like her name, was a light and vibrant person. She had even brightly stated that despite her faith, she had decided to remain single as long as reasonably possible.

I wanted to let Sanaa know that it was all right to see one hypnotherapist after another for the joy of exploration and the expansion of her mind. That said, it was not so necessary to manifest and hold onto her anxiety simply so that she could have a "reason" to see a hypnotherapist. Some people seek hypnotherapy, specifically to contact their spirit guides for guidance and answers. Yet here, Sanaa was annoyed with her spirit guides, believing their guiding words to be a bit too cliché for her. Presumably, what makes a cliché a cliché is a grain of some old truth that people keep repeating and referring back to, even after the original meaning is long forgotten or diluted with time.

"The guides are only here to help," I soothed Sanaa, hoping she might understand that ultimately, there was only one master in her life, herself. "You are the one who is going to decide how you'd like to be helped or not. If you'd like, we can send the guides away for now."

"I'm just so sick and tired of 'letting go' and 'focusing on the now,'" she replied bitterly. I did not know how Sanaa had become so sick and tired of letting go. But whatever process she chose to go through and how long the process needed to take would be entirely up to her.

So, we instructed the guides to back off. For now. And with the guides gone, I wished to establish something that could help Sanaa in her times of need. I reminded her of the timeless nature of her Inner Sanctuary and had the 19-year-old Sophia find her way to the sanctuary to meet with Sanaa.

In that safe space, when the two women quietly met face to face, the heartful beauty of the moment was tangible. "Whatever problem she's having," said Sophia in a softer and humbler tone than Sanaa's earlier. "It is not going to last forever. Sanaa can take one step at a time. There is no need to rush, no need for her to take each problem personally.

"And about her fear of travelling, she needs to realize how far she has come over the last few sessions. What is the worst that is going to happen? The worst is that she starts to feel weird. There are always people, and her guides, who are trained to help her if she only asks. Everything *will* work out. She will be fine. There is even this GPS in phones now. People don't even need to know where they are. Someone will find her…" Sophia trailed off, sobbing a little for Sanaa.

How does Sophia know about GPS? I marvelled at the timeless nature of the soul. Hearing those words from a past self, instead of from her guides, Sanaa finally accepted them. *It really doesn't matter who delivers the message, so long as the message was received.* Sophia was the right messenger for Sanaa, someone who could relate, who had felt extreme anxiety and self-doubt in the face of others' perspectives.

A foundation for unconditional acceptance existed between these two selves. Sophia could sense that Sanaa felt scared, alone, and not always sure of herself. In her soft, sweet voice, Sophia pointed out to Sanaa that Sanaa was fiercely independent, too; that she did not *want* people to help her for fear that she might get hurt if she let anyone get too close. Sanaa's protective layer had been revealed, showing the fortress wall that protected her vulnerability.

Out of the blue and eighteen months after Sanaa and Sophia had found a home in her Inner Sanctuary and mutual, unconditional acceptance of each other/herself, I received an email from Sanaa:

> Hi Kemila,
>
> This is Sanaa. You worked with me last year as I was trying to have a baby but had anxiety about being pregnant.
>
> I just wanted to thank you for all of your help in helping me with learning to trust myself more, letting go, and overcoming my fears to live in my present.
>
> Five months ago, I gave birth to a gorgeous baby girl! ☐I wouldn't have been able to do it without you. So, from the bottom of my heart, thank you!!
>
> A thousand blessings to you!
> Sanaa

Lost and Found

Events That Define Lives

Angela had an unconscious practice of answering questions with 'I guess…' A habit I quickly noted during our first session. It suggested that the pretty twenty-five-year-old, unsure of her mind, might have issues with self-doubt, but that was not what drew Angela to my practice. Angela was fascinated with experiencing a past life regression.

Originally from the lower mainland area of British Columbia, Angela had recently returned home after living and working abroad in London, England, for two years. "I did temp jobs and odd jobs. Anything I could find, really, to help keep me afloat," she explained from her seat on the couch across from me. "I guess the first time I even seriously entertained the idea of past lives and regression was when I arrived in London. I guess I felt a strong feeling of déjà vu in that city. Like I had been there before, even though I hadn't. So, when I got back to Vancouver, one of the first things I did was call a Past Life Regressionist. Even before I got a cell phone!" Angela said with a light and tinkly laugh.

In London, Angela also became clearer on her career prospects, opting to become an actress and, eventually, a film director. She had been considering this path for many years while working through her fear of losing herself and losing control. In the end, Angela found it an easy decision to make. I felt fortunate to learn Angela intended to become an actress; I love working with actors. I have found that anyone who can act generally possesses the ability to effortlessly go into hypnosis. And living and working in Vancouver, "Hollywood

North," I have had plenty of opportunities to work with them. Angela's eagerness and mine were a good match.

Being able to be hypnotized easily turned out to be true for Angela. It took less than three minutes for her to enter a past life scene and start to "see" things. Intriguingly, Angela was not relaxed. I tried lifting her arm. It was rigid. I asked her to relax her arm, and though she tried, Angela could not get it to relax. Surrendering her fears of losing control, of losing herself, was proving to be more of a "work in progress" than a done deal for the talented, young actress.

The life of a bored, disconnected, and aloof lawyer named Harry began to come through. We moved forward and backward in that twentieth-century English life. Nothing noteworthy occurred in that life; though bored and detached, Harry was consumed by what others thought of him, busily maintaining the image of 'the successful lawyer.'

Rather than seeking memorable events in that life, I decided to explore the boredom itself with Harry. But deep in this soul, something lay buried, and Harry could not recall the reason for his boredom. It sounds strange, but I have seen this in clients when a past life personality judges their life as boring. It is a judgment formed from the human perspective, not the soul's, and springs from self-denial and constrictive beliefs. Fantastically, life itself is never dull for the soul. It is always exciting because it is always the soul's choice for that lifetime. Souls, same as people, do not set out to do things they anticipate will be boring.

There are many ways to explore a traumatic, complex, or tedious lifetime, and one such way is to go to the moment right before death. When viewing a life from that unique vantage point, people often gain the detached clarity needed to discern their life's essential threads and patterns.

I brought Harry to the moment of his death. At seventy-eight, when asked to look back and reflect on his life, Harry discovered a crucial turning point in that life: his wife, Annabel, had been pulled under and carried away by a river's mighty current, and Harry had blamed himself for her drowning death. Things began to come into perspective for me then. It was almost as though the river had swept a piece of Harry's very self downstream along with his wife, resulting in him feeling dull and disconnected. It conributed hugely to his guilt. The brain will always attempt to protect itself from trauma and even from very dense emotions like guilt; Harry's guilt had buried the devastating event deep within the recesses of his mind. Suppressing his pain had allowed Harry to continue to function in the world after his wife's time, a world that had previously mattered so much to him. The constant self-doubt Angela was still exhibiting directly reflected Harry's guilt. Even her difficulty in articulating her reasons for wanting a past life regression, beyond "I guess, I am just drawn to it," derived from Harry's success in concealing his wounds.

For a short while after Harry's life reflection, I had Angela remain in a hypnotic state, allowing her time to remember everything she needed to know from her regression. Her two years in London had been an opportunity, on the soul level, to locate that missing piece of self. Now back home again, it was time to heal.

Every life and personality are akin to a single drop of water in a vast ocean; it is truest to itself and flows best when still connected to the greater whole. Unlike drops of water, humans develop fears and self-doubt when separated from their whole selves and can become stuck or stagnant. All the pain of survival comes from identifying with a part of self instead of appreciating the whole. Much like that drop of water, even a part of self is more than what we perceive it to be. The water droplet never stops *being* the ocean; we only perceive it as something separate when it is physically not *in* the ocean. Coming home to the ocean, the drop of water loses form, again flowing in constant harmony with the whole. The soul is like that, too; after death, in the non-physical realm, it ecstatically returns to the whole. Some call the 'whole' universal consciousness; others call it Allah, God, or Great Spirit, while others call it Source Energy or Source Love and Light. Whatever the name, the essence is the same, light and peace and love, and *that* essence is our true identity. Losing oneself and shedding a false identity can be like a soul returned to its source, not a loss but a transcendence. When a drop of water goes back to the ocean, it does not lose its identity. It finds its true identity of being the ocean. Only excitement and ecstasy await that moment of "loss."

I could appreciate why Angela's soul had chosen to be an actress in this lifetime. The joy and adventure of acting come, in part, from losing oneself in it, finding the rhythms and flow of a new character, of a different identity, and experiencing a world through their eyes. Parallel to acting, losing oneself is an ideal condition for channelling. Channelling is, in fact, one of the most natural states for us to be in on a soul level. What Angela feared the most might be the exact thing she needed most: to lose herself, a *false* sense of self.

With those parallels in mind, I guided Angela to use her channelling ability and become the drowned wife, Annabel.

The information transmitted more clearly than before. "When the current took me, I hit my head on a rock, and I knew it was just my time," Annabel confessed. "Harry must know that my death was quick. I did not suffer as he had after I was gone."

I asked Harry's wife, "You mean that life was meant to be a short one?"

"Yes. It was meant to happen so that I could move on to my next journey. My 'early' death was meant to happen so that Harry might learn the lesson he came to learn."

"Tell me more," I was eager to learn what Harry's life might be.

"Harry came here to discover and appreciate who he was in that life and all that he had; to be more present and connected. I drowned so that Harry might seize the opportunity to get in touch with himself, his true self, not the one he perceived through the eyes of others," Annabel said, concluding the channel.

The channel might have ended, but Angela remained in a creative, hypnotic state. I asked the would-be film director how she would adapt the movie's ending for Harry's life: "Instead of a long, tragic drama, I would make it a self-discovery movie," she began, rapidly conjuring up an alternate ending. "Annabel would still die at the same time by drowning in the river. But this time, Harry's busyness in keeping up with the status quo was upended by his wife's untimely death. It forces him to step back, take pause, and ponder the meaning of everything. And he starts to question his true purpose in life.

"After some comedic and heart-wrenching soul searching, Harry realizes *his* life was always about *him,* not what others thought of him. He redefines what success truly means to him and goes on to live a quiet but far from boring life.

He dies peacefully and contentedly at the age of seventy-eight, surrounded by flowers, those whose lives he touched—friends, family, business associates, and strangers—and of course, love." I closed my notebook, put my pen away, and inwardly smiled; *this Angela will make a stellar film director.*

That was one session four years ago, but I have met many a new client who has mentioned the starlet's name throughout the following years. Like Angela, most of them worked in the film industry. To this day, Angela still quietly refers new clients to me. Clients who share with me bits of who Angela is today. I am left feeling both grateful and happy to know that Angela has truly lost herself to find herself.

Many Blessings Will Come

Familial Healing

Lindsay telephoned my office one day, and straightaway, without posing a single question to me, she brusquely asked to book a Life-Between-Lives hypnosis session. "Between now and our appointment," I quickly added after scheduling her in. "If there are any questions that come up for you, please write them down and bring them with you for your session."

Our brief call left me with some questions for Lindsay: Had she ever had a Past Life Regression? Typically, I employ different methods to go to an inter-life regression, depending on if a client has previously had a past life regression. What were her plan and expectations for a Life-Between-Lives hypnotherapy session?

Some clients have many questions before they can decide about a session. Other people, like Lindsay, have zero questions or comments to make before making their decision. I would simply have to follow her lead and trust where the flow took us.

While very curt during our initial phone call, Lindsay opened up almost immediately upon arriving for our evening appointment. Now fifty years old, the semi-retired nurse with three surviving children had faced the loss of a great many loved ones in her life, and she was eager to understand why. Lindsay had suffered a miscarriage, followed by the abrupt loss of her son, Ricky. Ricky was only two-and-half-year-old at the time.

Three years before our meeting, Lindsay had also lost her twenty-year-old son, Daniel. And now the woman was grieving the loss of her husband, Doug, who had passed away three months earlier. She had cared for him at home during his last days, helping to ease her husband's transition from this life.

Though a spiritual person, she was now beginning to question life. Lindsay had always known death was not the end, but the pain of missing her life partner was still a great deal to bear. "I know Doug is fine somewhere, but he is not tangible. I can't see him, hear him, and touch him! Why do I have to go through the pain of losing him?" Lindsay pleaded and presented me with the three questions she had written down for our session:

> Why are there so many deaths in my life?
>
> Why did I have to go through the pain of losing a child three times?
>
> Where did they go?

Lindsay's only previous past life regression experience was in a group setting at her local library. But she loved Angel Card readings and did an excellent job of reading for others. Although, when it came to the nurse confronting her issues, Lindsay's readings did not work nearly as well.

"We are too close to ourselves to see ourselves clearly," I remarked. "Or maybe, you are just too good at second-guessing yourself?"

"Precisely," Lindsay willingly agreed. "Although, thinking of coming here this morning, I tried to pull an angel card. But no matter how hard I tried, I just couldn't even pull it. I found that very…" Instead of saying something like "disturbing," Lindsay reframed her thought and said, "…interesting." *Brilliant*, I thought.

I looked at Lindsay with my hypnotist's gaze and stated, "I know why."

"Why?" Lindsay asked, leaning forward and giving me her complete attention.

"Because you are supposed to do it here," I smiled.

"Really?" Her eyes widened with intrigue. "How?" Lindsay looked around, searching my office. *No, Lindsay, I don't have any angel cards here.*

"I am going to show you how," I instructed Lindsay to lean back on the recliner and close her eyes. "In your mind's eye, bring up a deck of angel cards," I paused briefly, allowing Lindsay to relax into the visualization process. "Now, shuffle the deck three times, just as you usually would. Then confidently and easily pull one card out."

"Ahhh!" Lindsay exclaimed, pleased. "It's a goddess card."

I intended to use whatever card Lindsay pulled as a guiding point to the realm she wished to visit.

"What does the goddess card say to you?"

"She says, 'Follow me!'"

"Do you trust her?"

"Yes!" Lindsay eagerly exclaimed.

"Even though you don't know where she may take you?"

"I'll follow her," Lindsay responded confidently. This was going much faster and smoother than even a hypnotist's speed. I silently thanked the Goddess for giving me such an incredible client, which had me feeling the rewards of my work.

"Now I'm going through yellow pulsating lights," Lindsay continued, "And the Goddess keeps looking back at me from time to time."

"To check and see if you are still following?" I queried.

"Yes."

"It seems she cares very much."

"Yes," Lindsay agreed in a voice tinged with tears.

"Ask her what her name is."

"Goddess Gwen..." she responded, then wavered. "Gwendolyn, Goddess Gwendolyn." A mass of people of every race and belief flew around in every direction, curiously looking at Lindsay. Goddess Gwendolyn beckoned for Lindsay to hurry up, the two ending up in a more expansive space. It was a space Lindsay remembered she had been to before she was born. A warm, golden, quivering light appeared again, and as Lindsay passed through it, she felt as though she were light itself.

Goddess Gwendolyn pointed, silently indicating they would proceed ahead to a grand building with pillars. The Goddess was bringing Lindsay to a premature life review. Usually, a life review happens *after* the death transition, like after a past life regression. However, Lindsay and I were not doing a past life regression; Lindsay was still Lindsay. Somehow, by following Goddess Gwendolyn, she had come to this in-between state.

"Life is not linear, Dear One," the Goddess said as Lindsay climbed the grand stairs and entered a vast hall with a colossal projection screen. Alone with the Goddess, Lindsay listened as the Goddess spoke of Lindsay's choices. As if on cue, the projection screen came to life. Both surprised and delighted, Lindsay watched as a cheerful little girl played with a young boy; it was Lindsay and her brother, Alfred.

"Connection," commented Lindsay, almost to herself. "When I was little, I was always happy when I was with my brother. Gwendolyn says that Alfred was also in some of my previous lives. I don't see him much now, though. He lives in California."

"Is this a message for you related to Alfred?"

"Gwendolyn tells me that it's time for me to go and see him. It's time for me to travel." The small but not insignificant life review seemingly finished, Lindsay again passed through the pulsing, yellow light.

"Can I ask her if I can go and see Doug?" Lindsay requested.

"Yes. Ask Gwendolyn."

Lindsay paused and then said, "She doesn't say anything."

"It's rare that she doesn't respond to you. Did she hear you?"

"She did turn around. But now she says, 'Come!'"

"Maybe there's a surprise for you. Just follow her."

The golden undulating glow came into view and shifted, swirling around, turning in on itself. Finally, the light settled, forming a beautiful, brilliant, pulsating heart. A man walked out through that throbbing, cosmic heart of light. Throwing a hand over her mouth, Lindsay gasped and burst into sobs of joy. The man was her husband, Doug, once again young and handsome.

"...Many blessings will come, Linds," Doug promised his wife. "You have already done so much in your life; created so many things. Now, it is time for you to see the many blessings coming your way. Always remember, Linds: LOVE is the *only* answer."

"Doug was *never* like this when he was alive," Lindsay told me. "He was always much more scientifically minded. He preferred facts and quantifiable things, empirical evidence. He didn't even believe in an afterlife; death was simply the end." Raw from sobbing, Lindsay paused to clear her throat before continuing. "I find it interesting, though. Why, after three months, would Doug tell me all these things now?" More than that, Lindsay wanted the answers to one of the questions she had come to the session with: *Where did Doug go when he died?*

"As of now, Linds. I am in a sort of healing centre. I might remain here for maybe another two months or so, in Earth time. After that, I am 'going fishing'", Doug said playfully and smiled at his wife. "And I will let you in on a little secret, too," he smiled again, "A good part of our little Ricky chose to come back to be our son, Mike."

"No wonder!" Lindsay exclaimed quietly to herself. "Mike always reminded me of Rick." Lindsay listened intently as her husband shared more insights about their extended family and children, like what kind of person Mike would likely marry. He urged Lindsay to pay for their son Mike, so he could go with her to visit Lindsay's brother in California; the other children could also go but would need to pay for themselves. Doug had seen their son, Daniel, a few times while visiting the 'healing centre.'

Lindsay took Doug's hand in hers. "It feels real," she happily reported to me. "It *is* real."

"As real as being tangible?" I was curious.

"Yes. I know he's not physically there, but I'm here with him."

"I wonder if Doug also went through a life review stage before arriving at the 'healing centre?' And if so, what were the lessons for his lifetime as Doug? Ask him now," I instructed Lindsay.

"Yes, he has," she said after a beat. "And it was all about love. Doug was learning that there is no 'dying,' so there is no need to fear it. My husband tells me not to even worry about 'stuff.' Not to worry about what's going on in the house or about setting goals. He tells me to simply take my time; don't rush into anything. And everything will work out."

Lindsay said to me wistfully, "I still want to know why there have been so many deaths in my life?"

"Ask Doug."

"You have *chosen* all those experiences," Doug answered. "I just came to play along. You forget that now." And he faded away to be replaced by the vast hall.

Lindsay watched the massive projection screen as it showed images of how she had chosen this life with the many deaths to experience loss; experiencing so many deaths had served to accelerate her growth. She remembered her soul had not reincarnated for quite a while and, on that soul level, had forgotten what it was like to lose in the physical realm.

Lindsay watched the projection receiving more information about the death of her son, Daniel. As it turned out, Daniel was a catalyst for awakening a great many young people. Daniel's spirit came to her. Overjoyed, Lindsay burst into tears and threw her arms around her son, cradling him in a huge hug.

"It's different here," Daniel told his mother through her tears. "It's not like Earth. Manifesting our desires is immediate. We fly wherever we want to go. We create whatever we want. Just think it, and we are there. You don't need money. Everybody is rich because they can immediately manifest what they need. There is no religion. I go to school here. Even though I was majoring in Commerce, I am really into music now."

"But where exactly are you?" Lindsay asked between ecstatic sobs.

"We are right beside you," Doug answered. "We can see you. We touch you, but you do not see us. Sometimes you feel us there. We are in the same place as you are but in different dimensions. Physical life on Earth is like a play, a big theatre. Everyone plays the roles they came to play. You knew all of this too. You just need to remember it," he ended sweetly, adding that themes of compassion played a significant role in Lindsay's life.

"I re-learned that many of my family members are in my soul group," Lindsay told me. "It's actually quite big!"

"If I were to visit your group today, what would you say to introduce the group to me?"

"I would tell you that my soul group and I are all teachers. We teach people how to remember their spiritual origin and cultivate awareness. Even though sometimes people don't appear to be listening, we share anyways. There is still an impact."

I like to tell my clients that I am a facilitator and that I am not here to agree or disagree with what they say, but in this case, I could not agree with Lindsay more. We all have an impact on others beyond what shows on the surface. If Lindsay's husband and son could change, in or out of time, so can anybody else.

In perfect synchronicity with my thoughts, a formless Doug repeated over and again until he was barely audible, to his wife and to all who would listen, *"Many blessings will come. Many blessings will come. Many blessings will come…"*

Epilogue

Remember Who You Are

We were approaching the end of Tania's fifth hypnotherapy session, and once again, I found myself being hypnotized into a trance by the cadence of my voice. The words I spoke, a part of the contextualization, spilt over and flowed like a dam that could no longer hold its floodwater: "… Get in touch with who you truly are from this moment on, because you have re-grown your wings, and you are becoming stronger now. And you know you can now do your nighttime meditation when you want to strengthen the connection with your guardian angel… So, when you think you go to bed at night, you actually go somewhere else, where you can fly and enjoy the ultimate freedom. That's the message you have received. The freedom is already there, without any need for others' validation, agreement, or approval. You can do what you want to do. You can choose what you want to choose. You can choose to love yourself. There is no way you cannot love yourself because *you* are love itself manifested as Tania. That is why it hurts so much when you don't love yourself enough. That is why you suffer when you crave other people's validation of you. Because to do so is to deny *who you are*.

"Now you know that which is you does not need anything. That is why you can receive everything. It's okay that sometimes you don't fit into human groups because you have all the animals following you anyways. You know animals are here to teach us unconditional love. That's why we humans want to follow animals. Now, animals are following you. That means you are not meant to "fit in" but to lead. You do not need to be "normal"; normal does not exist. You can only be natural. So, take a deep breath in, and allow the heavenly energy to sink into the core of your being.

"I will now count from zero to five," I instructed Tania. "At the count of five; eyes wide open; fully alert; awake; feeling wonderful in every way," and I counted to five to bring Tania out of a hypnotic state.

Tania was still lying on the couch. The moment her wide eyes popped open, she looked straight up at the ceiling. "I know you!" She proclaimed; her crystal-clear words projected from deep within her chest and sliced through the air. My heart trembled, but Tania continued: "I know you. When we went to the in-between-lives state, and you asked me who I saw before I was born, I didn't 'see' anyone. But when you were saying that last bit, I remembered your voice! That was the same voice that gave twenty of us a briefing before we were reincarnated. I remember the voice. And that is you!"

Tania was excited. She sat bolt upright now. "That voice," she gushed, enthused by her discovery, "I know it! You told us it can be a tough place to live on the Earth and to remember who we are. But you said it's okay. You will find us. Oh my God!"

Utterly floored, I could not recall any briefing of a group of souls/angels before they were born. Yet what Tania was saying made a great deal of strange sense to me. I never felt like I had chosen this profession, but that the profession had chosen me. But when being a hypnotherapist finally became my profession, I felt every ounce of my being cheering a giant, resounding, 'Yes!'

"I bet a lot of your clients these days are those angels," Tania added while neatly folding up the blanket she had just used. My mind quickly scanned the lengthy list of my clientele. Effortlessly, I singled out those people, those angels, and knew exactly who those people were. One of them was a young man I had met during a winter vacation in Hawaii, and we had a hypnosis session in my hotel room.

Two months earlier, Tania, an event organizer, came to see me for Past Life Regression, to resolve some intense emotional turmoil she had been experiencing. She had been to an Eye Movement Desensitization and Reprocessing (EMDR) practitioner for some work. To put her more troubling emotions to rest, the practitioner recommended that she see a hypnotherapist. Some graphicly disturbing images kept coming up during Tania's EMDR treatments: being helplessly thrown into a dumpster, bleeding to death, and being laughed at by a group of women after being gang-raped by a group of men. She believed those images to be glimpses of past lives.

I thought back to our first session and remembered being somewhat stunned by Tania's appearance. She had a small, slim body with a small face and large bright eyes almost disproportionate to her face, especially for an Asian like me. Tania looked like a human-ET hybrid, ethereal and exceptionally beautiful. She told me she had grown up being called "Ugly Monkey" and, of course, had believed it. In that initial session, I had called her "Angel" out of some unconscious knowing like a loving aunt might address her sweet, young niece. Tania had loved it.

We quickly established a connection, and at the end of our first appointment, Tania shared a sketch she had recently drawn. "I never knew how to draw," she confided. "But one day, I couldn't help but do this! I surprised myself that I could draw!" Her smartphone displayed a drawing of a fallen angel, sitting morosely in a corner, its wings broken. The angel was crying, and its tears watered a small plant at her feet as they fell to the earth. The image struck a chord within me that reverberated for some time.

After that first visit, we did several Past Life Regression sessions about four lifetimes on Earth riddled with abandonment, abuse, and powerlessness. Yet, in one life, she demonstrated a courageous warrior spirit and grace in the face of death. Tania came for her final session hoping to address her insecurity and challenges with an emotional obsession with her current relationship. So, we decided to view her origin, or her spirit essence, through a Life-Between-Lives Regression.

Tania travelled to a serenely beautiful nature setting: verdant green grasses, majestic trees, brilliant, sweet-scented flowers, and her deceased dog bounding out on large paws to greet her. She sat on a high cliff, overlooking the surrounding lands, and we knew her spirit's name as Anniel. I told Anniel that she could walk or fly when it was time to move from this pleasant place. Anniel walked, and her wings began to grow back as she walked through the meadow. She continued to walk, her wings continued to grow, and animals emerged from the forest to join her. In ever more significant numbers, all manner of animals came and began following her, an evolving angel. Anniel recognized that Guardian Angel of Animals was an aspect of her true identity.

We ventured down to a happily bubbling stream, where someone sat at its bank, smiling. It was Anniel's husband from one of her four Earth lives. His spiritual name was Marius, and Marius was there to guide and protect her. I took this opportunity to ask Anniel about Tania's current relationship: in that moment, her emotional obsession was no longer significant.

Capitalizing on Marius' loving and protective presence, I asked Anniel to test out flying with her new wings. Anniel eagerly obliged, happily again enjoying the freedom and beauty of flight. "Feel into who you are," I gently encouraged Anniel. "What feels natural and easy? Sometimes when we feel something is hard, it is because it's not natural for us. And when you are ready, move to the time just before Tania was reincarnated on the Earth… Allow yourself to know what happens when you decide to reincarnate on the Earth."

"I just raise my hand and then jumped peacefully into something," Anniel replied.

"What happened before you raised your hand? Was there any discussion?"

"There is a lineup with about twenty of us. We are told to take whatever is given. But I know whatever that is, I will handle it," the angel paused, thinking. "Now that I see it, maybe it was a little bit of a premature jump."

"Do you have a sense where the others from your group are now around the world?"

"No, I don't know. We did not have an agreement to connect with each other here on Earth."

"But somewhere along the way, you broke your wings. Do you remember what happened?"

"There was a lot of hardship and violence. A lot of not acknowledging or *accepting* who I am…" She trailed off. "I don't regret jumping in or volunteering," Anniel continued. "I remember now. It was all meant to happen. In a sense, I knew that when I jumped in. This is how I can grow. I am not supposed to fit in so that I can remember to love myself no matter what. Then I will know how to love others.

Because love is the only way." Tania-Anniel took a long, deep, restorative breath. "The way to love yourself is to remember who you are," she concluded.

I thank Tania and all the angels I am blessed to have worked with for helping me remember who *I* am.

Acknowledgements

Writing a book, like anything, takes a village. I am truly honoured and touched by all my amazing clients whose healing, spiritual exploration, and travelling experiences inspired the writing of this book! It is a great joy and high honour to journey with you and support your continued growth and self-realization.

I have blogged about a few of these cases on my website throughout my years of working and writing. But it has been another kind of journey putting them together into a book. And for that part, good editors come into play. I first want to thank Sandra Nomoto for putting the stories together for me and for her timely delivery of an organized manuscript. Her professionalism and understanding of this subject matter have afforded me a good deal of ease while joggling my busy practice and putting together this book, Manny Blessings Will Come.

I am forever grateful to my partner, Tim Melanchuk, for going through this book several times and wordsmithing the parts that I was so burning to say but could not find a better way to express. I courageously said some of them awkwardly, and you turned them into something both accurate and eloquent.

I am genuinely awed by my dedicated editor, Melanie Christian. Your thorough approach and your way of asking the best questions have made this book the complete version of itself. You have brought such a flow, clarity, and poetry to my words, and as my partner put it, they have made me a better writer. I am so glad we met.

Made in the USA
Monee, IL
17 September 2022